After New Labour

Social Theory and Centre-Left Politics

Will Leggett

Lecturer in Sociology, University of Birmingham

palgrave
macmillan

First published in 2005 by
PALGRAVE MACMILLAN
Houndmills, Basingstoke, Hampshire RG21 6XS and
175 Fifth Avenue, New York, N.Y. 10010
Companies and representatives throughout the world.

PALGRAVE MACMILLAN is the global academic imprint of the Palgrave
Macmillan division of St. Martin's Press, LLC and of Palgrave Macmillan Ltd.
Macmillan® is a registered trademark in the United States, United Kingdom
and other countries. Palgrave is a registered trademark in the European
Union and other countries.

ISBN-13: 978–1–4039–4658–4 hardback
ISBN-10: 1–4039–4658–2   hardback
ISBN-13: 978–1–4039–4659–1 paperback
ISBN-10: 1–4039–4659–0   paperback

This book is printed on paper suitable for recycling and made from fully
managed and sustained forest sources.

A catalogue record for this book is available from the British Library.

Library of Congress Cataloging-in-Publication Data

Leggett, Will.
    After new Labour : social theory and centre-left politics / Will
Leggett.
        p. cm.
    Includes bibliographical references and index.
    ISBN 1–4039–4658–2 (cloth) – ISBN 1–4039–4659–0 (paper)
        1. Social change. 2. Right and left (Political science). 3. Labour Party
(Great Britain). I. Title.
HM831.L44 2005
306.2′0941—dc22   2005046328

10 9 8 7 6 5 4 3 2 1
14 13 12 11 10 09 08 07 06 05

Printed and bound in Great Britain by
Antony Rowe Ltd, Chippenham and Eastbourne

For my parents

Contents

Acknowledgements

The research leading to this book was funded by the Economic and Social Research Council. Chapter 3 draws on my article, 'Social change, values and political agency: the case of the Third Way', in *Politics*, 24:1 (2004) published by Blackwell. I am grateful to numerous friends and colleagues for their engagement and support. Special thanks are due to Luke Martell, Phil Larkin and Alan Finlayson. And most of all to Jo – for showing me that there definitely *is* life after New Labour.

Introduction

New Labour has swept all before it. The old left and the Conservatives appear to have no answer to its Third Way brand of modernising social democracy. Even in the face of a deeply unpopular war in Iraq and mounting disputes over his domestic agenda, Tony Blair comfortably won a historic third term with an 'unremittingly New Labour' manifesto. But New Labour is not loved. It has no depth of support. We cannot identify a Blairite or Third Way voter in the way we could spot a supporter of, say, Mrs Thatcher. The enduring question asked of New Labour may well be: how could a social democratic party dominate British politics so comprehensively, for so long, but fail to entrench a progressive cultural shift in British society? Only at the end of its second term did New Labour wake up to the need to forge, in Gordon Brown's words, a 'progressive consensus' to secure its legacy. But does it have the intellectual resources to do it? This book argues that the framework of the Third Way *does* offer the basis for an enduring centre-left narrative. But for this to be genuinely progressive, Third Way thinking needs to re-engage with some of the insights provided by its many critics on the left.

So this is not another book about what New Labour or the Third Way 'is'. Is it Thatcherism mark II? Is it in the 'Old Labour' tradition? Is it progressive? Authoritarian? Is it all spin? Is it Blair's project – or Brown's? Nor is this a commentary on what New Labour has done in government, or a discussion of specific policies. Instead, the book develops a particular approach to analysing New Labour's Third Way, with a view to uncovering more progressive possibilities beyond it. In so doing, it also offers the first detailed analysis of the Third Way's left critics.[1]

1

Specifically, the Third Way is understood here as what we might call a 'sociological' political project. It is based on claims about a changed world and how the centre-left – and all of us – must adapt to it. Given this, endless arguments over what constitute 'real' Labour values are unhelpful. Instead, it is important to understand the *relationship between* the Third Way's sociological claims and the role of political values. What are the implications of social change for our understanding of left and right? Must political strategies merely respond to wider social processes such as globalisation – or does there remain a space for politics to steer them? These issues are significant for thinking through the future of the centre-left, broadly conceived, regardless of the immediate political fortunes of New Labour.

In approaching the New Labour 'problem' in this way, the book has both a theoretical and a political aim. Theoretically, it explores the nature of political strategising in an age of rapid social transforma-tion. Politically, it looks towards a more progressive narrative for the centre-left, one that resonates with social experience and can inspire support for a progressive consensus. The much-maligned Third Way has thus far failed to achieve this task. However, it does offer us a use-ful sociological diagnosis of contemporary politics – and how the left should react to it. For this reason, the book places an engagement with the Third Way – and its critics – at the centre of the analysis. The rest of this introduction discusses the significance of the Third Way and outlines in detail the structure and arguments of the book.

Taking the Third Way seriously

The emergence of the Third Way

During a sustained period of Anglo-American neoliberal electoral success in the 1980s and 1990s, the British Labour Party and US Democrats embarked on a process of modernisation in a bid to halt their electoral decline. This led to the emergence of the New Democrats under the leadership of Bill Clinton and New Labour under Tony Blair. A similar reformist debate developed within a number of European social democratic parties, most notably the German SPD, as well as further afield in countries such as New Zealand and Brazil. Modernising centre-left leaders sought a 'big idea' to provide ideolog-ical coherence to their political projects, and Blair famously flirted with notions of both communitarianism and stakeholding.[2] However, it was the Third Way that emerged as the self-styled governing philosophy of the centre-left: the outcome of, and vehicle for continuing, its process of modernisation. The Third Way is premised on a critique of the first two 'ways': on the one hand, what it identifies as the 'old left', consisting of socialism (generically conceived) and postwar Keynesian social democracy, and on the other the New Right neoliberalism of the 1980s and 1990s. The Third Way is an attempt to synthesise what is held to be positive about these two previous traditions, while rejecting their negative aspects. Third Wayers support the commitment of social democracy to equality of opportunity and social justice, and see an important role for government in delivering them. However, the old left is criticised for being overly statist, stifling innovation and neglecting individual aspiration. Consequently, Third Wayers acknowledge the neoliberal emphasis on the dynamic role of markets in generating innovation and individual responsibility. At the same time, the extreme neoliberal belief in universal market solutions is rejected, as it fails to understand the need for active government and threatens social cohesion. This search for a synthesis is summarised in Blair's own early characterisation of the Third Way, as a quest for 'a way of marrying together an open, competitive and successful economy with a just, decent and humane society'.[3]

Style over substance?

The Third Way is often criticised for being nothing but spin: an electoral marketing device. But the choice of the specific label 'Third Way' to describe the modernised ideology of the centre-left may well go down as one of the most ill-judged pieces of political marketing in history. That it should have been adopted by supposed masters of political language, such as Bill Clinton and Tony Blair, as well as a savvy academic entrepreneur like Anthony Giddens, makes it all the more baffling. The term has been derided since its inception, consistently written off or pronounced as dead by New Labour's critics, and gradually removed from the party's own public rhetoric. The then Conservative leader William Hague captured a common sentiment, when he ridiculed Blair's attempt to encourage his views upon the French parliament: 'On Monday you gave the French the third way. On Wednesday they gave you the two fingers.'[4] Nevertheless, this book continues to refer to the Third Way. It is the closest thing to a governing ideology of the centre-left, with far greater coherence than its critics grant. When the Third Way was at its political height at the turn of this century, with numerous centre-left governments signed up to its key tenets, Giddens noted that it had become 'a worldwide phenomenon that almost all centre-left parties have reconstructed their doctrines in response to'.[5] Despite subsequent electoral setbacks for the centre-left, Blair reiterated in 2003 that 'The Third Way banner has successfully established itself as a central point of reference in debates on the future of the Centre Left from continental Europe to Brazil and even China.'[6] Speaking in the same year Bill Clinton, the original 'Third Wayer', went further by suggesting that the 'The Third Way should be the dominant mode of thinking about change in the 21st century.'[7] So while the centre-left seek to update their thinking to deal with issues such as global security or the challenge of neo-conservatism, and whatever the next sobriquet for their approach (for example, 'progressive governance', or Giddens' preferred 'neo-progressivism'),[8] this will reflect a decade of Third Way thinking that constitutes an extensive body of theoretical and policy work, among both academics and political practitioners. However, perhaps the best indication of the entrenchment and significance of the Third Way is the continuing attention paid to it by its *critics*, who lie at the heart of this study. This is illustrated by Callinicos who, from a Marxist perspective, has devoted a book to the Third Way in which he claims to have 'tried to take it seriously on its own terms. Even where its proponents' arguments are thin and weak, as is very often the case, they touch on genuinely important issues.'[9] Similarly, the assumption of this book is that to consider the future of New Labour, or any other part of the centre-left, demands an engagement with Third Way ideas.

Analysing New Labour's Third Way – and its critics

A significant literature on the Third Way has developed over the years of the Blair administration. These range from the high minded (*The Third Way to the Good Society*), through the technical ('Is there a Third Way in labour law?') to the exotic ('Third Way on the beach').[10] Some contributions seek to directly elaborate (or criticise) Third Way theory.[11] More typically, others offer general commentaries upon New Labour and social democracy, which frequently incorporate an account of the Third Way as part of their analysis.[12] Related to these are policy-focused contributions; these tend to either seek evidence of an overall Third Way approach emerging from policy programmes, or advocate a Third Way for a particular policy area.[13] The writings and speeches of Third Way politicians try to give theoretical coherence to the Third Way project as it unfolds in practice. Such output is joined by other interventions, including think-tank reports and several edited collections, all variously concerned with social change and/or centre-left politics – these may or may not explicitly seek to elaborate the Third Way. Academic and other commentary *about* the Third Way provides the material for my examination of responses to it. Given the constant interaction between academic, political and journalistic actors, commentaries about the Third Way cannot be clearly separated from the elaboration of the project itself.[14]

From these various sources, the two main approaches to analysing the Third Way emerge as those which are ideas-based, and those which focus more on social and political opportunities and constraints. The former type tries to define the Third Way, its origins and possible futures, by locating it in the context of existing ideological traditions and categories. Given that the Third Way makes claims to being a modernised social democracy, it is against the benchmark of a perceived social democratic orthodoxy that it is most commonly assessed. In particular, there has been considerable debate as to whether the Third Way is indeed a departure from a more traditional Labour position. Approaches which focus on the social and political context are largely agreed over the contours of the changed operating environment the Third Way claims to inhabit. However, key arguments emerge over the extent to which environmental changes *necessitated* the emergence of the Third Way, and in the particular form that it has taken. It is at this juncture that ideas-based and more empirical approaches to the Third Way overlap, as analysts try to assess the extent to which it is an *ideologically* driven project, or a *pragmatic* response to changing circumstances. Both types of analysis are important to understanding the Third Way. However, where current approaches have variously discussed the Third Way's values and (to a lesser extent) sociological dimensions, this book identifies the *relationship* between the two as vital to both grasping its political character, and developing possible alternatives.

Third Way ideas have a global reach and are not reducible to a single administration or thinker. However, the book's implicit reference points are domestic aspects of the New Labour administration.

There are important historical reasons for this. New Labour's political trajectory is grounded in a fairly parochial set of debates among the British Left; these date back to the 1980s and the problem of how the left should respond to Thatcherism (see Chapter 7). Having emerged on a terrain shaped by a sustained neoliberal experiment, New Labour above all centre-left parties can claim to know the political effects of both of the first two 'ways'. Of course, the US was also dominated by neoliberals in the 1980s. Indeed, the political beginnings of the Third Way can be clearly traced to Bill Clinton's political response to this situation from within the modernising Democratic Leadership Council, prior to his election to president in 1992.[15] However, it was only in the UK that the neoliberal project involved an explicit assault on the ideology, institutions and practices of an 'old left'; there was no equivalent target for assault in the US. A further reason for focusing on New Labour is that, of all the centre-left leaders, Blair has been the most explicit in his attempts to elaborate a Third Way governing philosophy. This has included the publication of a pamphlet on the subject in his name, the encouraging of the Third Way approach upon other centre-left leaders and attempts to explain the concept to the wider public in keynote speeches.[16] Blair's interest in the Third Way has been mirrored in the various intellectual influences on New Labour, and among political analysts in British academia. The most obvious of these is sociologist Anthony Giddens, who has tried to directly link his wider Third Way theory to a programmatic outline for New Labour.[17] It has also included think-tanks such as Demos, the Fabian Society, the Institute for Public Policy Research and, more recently, Compass. All of these have maintained an interest in the Third Way as a cohering idea for the New Labour project.

In considering New Labour as a Third Way exemplar throughout the book, there is no discussion of foreign policy, or the geopolitical stage that Blair has been so prominent on since 2001. In a book devoted to Blair's personal legacy, or the record of New Labour in office, such an omission would clearly be unacceptable. Doubtless there are debates to be had about the extent to which New Labour's (or, more specifically, Blair's) foreign policy can be framed in terms of debates about the Third Way. But, on this issue, I largely share Giddens' view that 'The Third Way is not some kind of formula that can be applied to any circumstance; it is a debate about left revisionism. Therefore, it has nothing to say on the rights and wrongs of war in Iraq.'[18] The questions addressed by the Third Way – about how fundamental social changes such as globalisation and individualisation affect the centre-left – predate 9/11, the Iraq conflict and the 'war on terror'. They remain strongly relevant to both domestic and (ultimately) international politics, despite the new prominence of global security issues.

In sum, the book is based on three analytical premises that flow from one another. First, the Third Way is treated as primarily a sociological project. On this perspective, the Third Way is not based upon an enduring ideological tradition, or a set of *a priori* philosophical or political-theoretical claims. Rather, the starting point of Third Way theory is a set of claims about the nature of a changed world, and the implications of such change for politics in general and the centre-left in particular. The second premise is that to understand the political character of the Third Way requires analysis of the relationship between its sociology and its values. Thirdly, on the basis of this analysis, it is possible to identify alternative trajectories for the Third Way, and to reconstruct it as a political project.

The structure of the book

Any of the book's chapters can be read in isolation, but together they take the form of a structured argument built up in three parts. Part I identifies the sociological and value dimensions of the Third Way and, most importantly, constructs a model of the relations between them. On the basis of this model, Part II examines critical responses to the Third Way from the left. Part III then develops these critiques into the theoretical basis for a reconstructed, more progressive centre-left project, some key themes of which are outlined.

Part I – When Sociology Met Politics: New Labour and the Third Way

Chapter 1 examines the Third Way as a sociological project, based upon claims about social changes with radical implications for politics. These begin with Giddens' macro sociology, which discusses processes such as globalisation, individualisation and detraditionalisation as comprising a new era of reflexive modernity. The chapter then examines the more specific themes of economic globalisation; work and identity; and work and welfare. In each case, the implications of social change for the categories of left and right are examined. I suggest that there are three types of claim made in this respect, each with different implications for political agency. There are those which imply an *undermining* of left and right, those which *reconfigure* their meaning and, consequently, those that actively *recombine* them in the reconfigured political space. Suggestions that social change undermines left and right minimise the options for political intervention. However, in a newly reconfigured political space there is room for Third Wayers to actively recombine left and right, in an attempt to differentiate themselves from both.

Chapter 2 discusses attempts to develop a set of Third Way values that distinguish it as a distinctive political philosophy, alongside its sociological claims. This normative agenda implies a strong degree of political agency and emphasises political leadership. However, it also underplays the structural constraints posited by Third Way sociology. In particular, commentators on the Third Way have tended to assess its normative claims against an enduring left/right axis of political philosophies. This neglects how the social forces giving rise to the Third Way are held to have made the left/right framework redundant, or at least radically reconfigured.

Chapter 3 examines the *relationship* between the sociological and normative elements of the Third Way. I suggest that Third Wayers make four types of claim concerning this relationship, each again involving different degrees of latitude for political agency. The first sees values as merely a functional, mechanical response to social change, and thus allows the least room for politics. The second type sees values as being enduring but updated to meet the demands of new times. The third type identifies a historical confluence between enduring values and contemporary circumstances. Finally, a value-led approach sees values as steering social change and thus allows the most room for political leadership. I argue that each of these positions is inadequate for developing a successful political strategy. At the extremes, the sociological determinism of the functionalist approach obliterates the space for politics, while the value-led approach neglects the sociological context within which the Third Way operates. Any reconstruction of the Third Way needs to engage with the social transformations which frame it *and* manipulate the continuing space for politics to develop social change in more progressive directions.

Part II – The Left Critics

Part II examines the Third Way's left critics against the same criteria that the Third Way itself was analysed in Part I: how do they interpret the social conditions that frame contemporary politics?; what are the implications for the categories of left and right?; and how do they assess the relations between social change and the development of political values? For analytical purposes, the critics are divided into three broad categories, with a chapter devoted to each. However, few individual critics sit straightforwardly in one category; they often appear in more than one chapter and may not self-identify with the particular label I assign them. Nevertheless, the categories do serve to capture the key criticisms the Third Way has received from the left.

To this end, Chapter 4 examines neo-Marxist responses, which see the Third Way as the latest political attempt to manage an enduring system of exploitative, capitalist economic and social relations. Chapter 5 identifies a disparate set of perspectives under the label of 'anti-technocrats'. In the tradition of Foucauldian analysis of governmentality, as well as Frankfurt School critical theory, this group is united by its treatment of the Third Way as a specific mode of governance. Where neo-Marxists tend to conceive of the Third Way as a project to reconfigure capitalist social relations, anti-technocrats understand it as embodying the development of a technocratic, instrumentalist reason that seeks to extend governance across social life. This involves reconfiguring the relations between the state, economy and citizen, and may overlap with the project of capitalist expansion identified by neo-Marxists. Chapter 6 examines social democratic responses to the Third Way. These are particularly significant because they operate on the same political terrain as the Third Way itself, given that Third Wayers frequently describe their own project as modernised social democracy.

Part III – After New Labour

The final part of the book outlines a theoretical approach to developing centre-left strategies, which is used to progressively reconstruct key Third Way themes. Chapter 7 synthesises the strengths and weaknesses of the Third Way's critics. They are criticised for replicating the Third Way's understanding of left/right and the relations between social change and political agency. The critics thus fail to both recognise changed social conditions, or to show how political action can mould them progressively. However, the critics have two main strengths: they can link political projects to material interests and, consequently, maintain a left/right distinction in terms of a critique of the commodification of social life. A disparate, 'cultural critique' of the Third Way has the potential to overcome the weaknesses of the left responses discussed. Drawing on both neo-Gramscian and post-Marxist theories, this critique recognises the importance of social change in framing political strategies, but also perceives such change as open-ended and subject to political intervention. However, the cultural critique's focus on the fluidity of social forms makes it reluctant to specify programmatic outcomes. Instead, cultural critics call for the opening out of political spaces through democratisation. I argue that this should be given a more substantive content by drawing on the strengths identified in the more traditional left perspectives: a critique of social commodification and a defence of a left/right dichotomy on this basis.

Chapter 8 reconstructs three key Third Way themes – individualisation, community and modernisation – using the approach developed in Chapter 7. Third Way theory presumes and encourages a commodified, atomised view of the individual who is constrained by a culturally conservative community. It presents modernisation as a neutral, external imperative which individuals and communities must adapt to, while in practice it fulfils highly ideological functions. In contrast, a more developmental view of individualisation as autonomy is identified, complemented by a more progressive reading of community as the site of individual empowerment. Modernisation is recast as the explicitly political process with which to achieve these ends. For this new narrative to be distinctively of the left, it needs to maintain a critique of how commodification distorts a more progressive sense of individualisation and community. Vitally, it also needs to offer a substantive vision of the type of society that modernisation processes are aimed at creating. The result could be a centre-left project that remains in touch with the sociological challenges identified by the Third Way, but that has the capacity to inspire support for converting them into progressive outcomes.

Part I

When Sociology Met Politics: New Labour and the Third Way

1
Third Way Sociology

This book is premised on the view that Third Way analysis, which has informed New Labour and other modernising social democratic parties, is essentially *sociological*. It is no coincidence that the leading Third Way intellectual, Anthony Giddens, is a sociologist. The Third Way is not based primarily on political-philosophical claims about what makes the 'good society'. Instead it is derived from an account of large-scale, rapid social transformations that the centre-left must adapt to, with globalisation being the most significant. Of course, this does not mean that Third Way politicians (or even sociologists!) do not have values, or ideas about how they think society *ought* to be. There has been a protracted debate about what constitutes New Labour values, and Blair and others often claim that their project is value-driven (see Chapter 2). But there is no doubt that the impulse behind Third Way theory and rhetoric is a belief that the world is changing in ways that call into question some of our most basic political assumptions. Claims of this type are nothing new; the political analyses of, for example, nineteenth-century sociologists such as Marx and Durkheim were based on the dilemmas posed by a rapidly emerging industrial capitalism. But, from the outset, the Third Way's appeal to a changed world has been particularly acute. As Driver and Martell stressed, in the first major academic analysis of New Labour in office, 'For Labour modernizers, the idea of new times underpins the whole New Labour project. In a changing world, new means are required to deliver old ends.'[1]

While it is widely acknowledged that modernising centre-left parties are self-consciously a response to a 'changed world', surprisingly few analysts focus in detail on how this sociological approach frames the theory, values, policies and strategy of the Third Way.[2] By contrast, this book argues that understanding the significance and role of Third Way sociology is vital to grasping its political character, and to developing any viable alternative. In particular, the importance of analysing the *relationship between* the sociological assumptions of the Third Way, its values and what this implies for political agency, is a central theme. The aim of this opening chapter is not to test the empirical veracity of the Third Way's sociological analysis. Instead, the focus is on how Third Way claims regarding a changed world are held to impact upon political possibilities, in terms of the categories of left and right. At different times the Third Way has claimed to be between left and right, to have combined them or even moved beyond them. How does Third Way sociology lead to these claims – and what do they tell us about the possibility of *any* kind of political interventions under contemporary conditions? The answers to these questions can both help us understand the Third Way – and think through alternatives.

The discussion begins with an overview of the most general level of Third Way social theory, primarily in the work of Giddens. It then moves on to the Third Way account of social change in three specific areas: economic globalisation; work and identity; and work, welfare and exclusion. In each case, three types of implication for the categories of left and right are identified: their undermining, reconfiguration and recombination, each implying a different degree of room for political manoeuvre. The *undermining* of left/right follows from a view that these categories were tied to a particular social formation. This formation has now been overhauled by dramatic social change which limits the steering potential of politics. The *reconfiguring* of left/right means that 'old' left/right positions are now best described by some other device, such as libertarian/authoritarian or radical/ conservative. This opens up new spaces for political projects such as the Third Way. It is within such spaces that the *recombination* of left/right occurs. This implies that the themes of the left-right axis have remained intact, but that Third Way actors are mixing them in new ways. Such an approach is evident in Third Wayers' frequent use of 'and' – e.g. efficiency *and* fairness, rights *and* responsibilities – in order to differentiate themselves from the 'old' either/or politics of traditional socialism and social democracy, as well as the neoliberal right.

The macro social theory of the Third Way

Undermining of left and right

It is striking how the leaders of the three main UK political parties are increasingly reluctant to describe themselves as being either on the left or right, pointing to how such labels are apparently outdated, or no longer reflect the concerns of 'ordinary people'. New Labour politicians and Third Way theorists have led this tendency, with their frequent – although not consistent – claims that social change has consigned left and right to history. Recounting his objective on being elected as Labour Leader in 1994, Blair suggested that he wanted to explain how:

> we could get beyond the traditional boundaries of right and left, and you could have a pro-business, pro-enterprise but pro-fairness political party. We have to create a different type of progressive, political force, which has left the redundant twentieth-century battles between capitalism and communism behind.[3]

Similarly, in answering his own question, *Why Vote Labour?*, prior to the 1997 general election, Labour MP Tony Wright suggested that the new politics 'is an agenda for a world that has put the old sterile ideological divides behind it'.[4] These bold statements about the redundant old politics of left and right reflect Third Way social theory, identifying revolutionary social changes that render obsolete many of the assumptions, and solutions, offered from within left/right parameters. This translates into the strongest claims that Third Way politics amounts to a *transcendence* of traditional notions of left and right. From this perspective, prior to any concrete Third Way programme, the ideological ground had to be cleared. This involved showing that the other 'ways' – socialism and traditional social democracy from the left, and conservatism and neoliberalism from the right – were defunct, and a third way necessary. As Rustin notes:

> Strategies defining themselves as a third or middle way characteristically proceed by castigating the received options to both left and right. The hope is that disillusion with existing and sometimes weary antagonisms, can be channelled into belief in a new untarnished alternative.[5]

The most comprehensive method of writing off the first two 'ways' was to show that history itself had undermined the very left–right axis that underpinned them. In his *Beyond Left and Right* (1994), Giddens set about this task by identifying what he calls 'the social revolutions of our time'. These are held to explain the demise of left and right, and have continued to underpin Giddens' elaboration of Third Way politics.[6] The key process Giddens points to, from which the others flow, is *globalisation*. Communications technologies have led to a stretching of global social relations, with the effect that all local action has global social consequences. This is about more than just a quantitative change, in terms of increasing the extent of global interactions. It also involves a qualitative shift in the nature of social relations, with increasing interaction and information flows leading to a 'global cosmopolitanism'. Through this, we experience the second revolution: *detraditionalisation*. With the proliferation of information and the visibility of a range of lifestyle choices, institutions and practices can no longer justify themselves through traditional means. Pre-given authority symbols, such as claims to religious or ideological universalism, no longer convince. Instead, in the context of the proliferation of knowledge claims, existing practices are forced into a dialogic relationship: they must justify themselves on the basis of reasoned argument. This leads Giddens to a definition of *fundamentalism* as traditions that refuse such dialogic engagement, and continue to justify themselves self-referentially.

The third and fourth social revolutions result from the loosening of traditional structural constraints that detraditionalisation brings about. *Individualisation* is presented as a decline of collective attachments and the increasing desire for individual autonomy. This process occurs as, in the face of the retreat of traditional practices, identity becomes a matter of active self-creation. Individualisation itself occurs against the backdrop of *social reflexivity*.[7] Reflexivity refers to the ability of agents, on the basis of a proliferation of information about the social world, to constantly filter that information. In so doing, they can act in a way that influences the conditions for future reflection and action. The ongoing process of social reflexivity results in the fifth transformation: the shift to *manufactured uncertainty*. Modern societies have reached a stage where, often as a result of our own previous interventions into the social and natural worlds, the precise nature and scale of the risks we confront have become incalculable (e.g. with regard to global warming, or the effect of GM foods).[8] In the context of such uncertainty, it is no longer possible to perceive a single, universally correct course of action as part of a linear story of social progress.

What is the relationship between these social revolutions and the decline of the categories of left and right? Giddens' premise is that the rigid left/right dichotomy becomes incapable of serving as a consistent guide for political action. In the detraditionalised context, claims to a monopoly on political truth (such as socialism) are rejected as a form of fundamentalism. Reflexive, informed subjects – individualised from binding structural constraints – are resistant to political projects that attempt to construct identities from above. In the climate of manufactured uncertainty, in which outcomes are seen as open-ended, teleological theories of historical development (such as communism) are similarly rejected. The Grand Narratives of left and right lose their descriptive and prescriptive power in a society which is sceptical about totalising projects.

Giddens' account of the 'social revolutions of our time' provides a general theory of the conditions undermining left and right, paving the way for a Third Way politics that seeks to move beyond them. The suggestion that social change has made left and right virtually obsolete leaves little room for active political interventions. In his description of a world beyond left and right, Giddens gives the Third Way the appearance of functional and historical inevitability: it emerges as the only logical outcome in the epochal shift from what he describes as 'simple' to 'reflexive' modernity.[9] However, we see below how accounts of the social conditions necessitating a Third Way do not remove left and right from the equation altogether. The undermining of left and right also results in the *reconfiguration* and active *recombination* of the elements associated with each.

Reconfiguration of left and right: radicals and conservatives

In attempting to define the enemy of his political project, Blair has spoken of the 'forces of conservatism' on left and right who are holding back the modernisation of Britain.[10] While dismissed by many as opportunist politicking, the attack on such 'forces' is entirely consistent with Third Way theory. With the alleged undermining of left and right, the characteristics that have been associated with them are reconfigured. In Third Way commentaries, this is manifested in a shift from talking about left and right to describing radicals and conservatives. Marquand suggests that from the time of the French Revolution, the categorisation of left and right had implied that the left was the radical force, favouring social and political change, while the right conservatively opposed it. The left was always seen as progressive because change itself was regarded as inherently emancipatory. In contrast to this clear left/right distinction, the political centre was ambiguous and undecided.[11]

Marquand, and later others such as Giddens, argue that the sociologically driven decline of left/right has exploded this view. Today's radicals are those who have embraced the social revolutions of our time, whereas the conservatives are those who resist them. There is nothing new there, except that the assumption that it is the left who are radical and progressive has been abandoned. Not having engaged with social change, the left are attached to practices that are disintegrating, or have lost their radical impetus. In Giddens' words, ' "Radicalism" cannot any longer be equated with "being on the left." On the contrary, it often means breaking with established leftist doctrines where they have lost their purchase on the world.'[12] The most illustrative example is the welfare state. With the left forced into a defensive position over welfare, it finds itself sharing ground with traditional conservatives, in the sense of seeking to defend old practices in the face of new times. As Marquand puts it:

> It is a moot point whether the most conservative, change-fearing and change-opposing is the hard left, what remains of the old-fashioned, blue-collar Labour right or the equally demoralised remnants of traditional, *noblesse-oblige* Tory paternalism.[13]

On this view, political radicalism came to be represented by neoliberalism, which aligned itself with the social changes identified by Giddens, Marquand and others. These changes included the rise of individualisation and the redundancy of command and control systems of decision-making. In this context, a neoliberal philosophy – based on individual liberty and the primacy of market mechanisms – resonated with the leading edge of social change. This reconfiguration of left and right, portraying the 'old left' as a conservative force and recognising the radical, even progressive elements of neoliberalism, opened up new political spaces. It was within such spaces that the Third Way was developed against both the old left and New Right.

Recombination of left and right: the Third Way

The account of the undermining and reconfiguring of left/right could lead to the view that it is *neoliberalism* which represents a 'third way'; this is the conclusion of many of the Third Way's leftist critics described in Part II. Neoliberalism, after all, found a way through both Keynesian social democracy and one-nation conservatism; both of these positions had become outmoded through being tied to a post-war welfare state which was unravelling. However, the Third Way is, of course, supposed to remain anchored in the centre-*left*. To do so, it clearly cannot align itself fully with neoliberal ideas, and has to preserve a link to its social democratic heritage. As Blair puts it, 'The Third Way is not an attempt to split the difference between Right and Left. It is about traditional values in a changed world.'[14] Giddens concurs, subtitling his original book on the Third Way, 'The renewal of social democracy' and increasingly emphasising its social democratic credentials in subsequent years.[15] For the new social terrain to appear as an opportunity for the centre-left, it had to be demonstrated that they had a narrative with which they could claim the new world. In Blair's words, 'Just as economic and social change were critical to sweeping the Right to power, so they were critical to its undoing. The challenge for the Third Way is to engage fully with the implications of that change.'[16] The task for the centre-left was to ensure that they had embraced the new times, by having moved on from Keynesian social democracy, but in a way that was distinct from the neoliberals whose doctrines had failed to maintain social cohesion. It was in this space that the Third Way emerged as an attempt to actively *recombine* elements of both old left and New Right.

At the most theoretical level, Giddens suggests that the reconfiguration of left and right implies a role for a 'philosophic conservatism'. Drawing on conservative philosophers like Oakeshott, Giddens criticises the 'radicalism' of both the old left and New Right: each have a dogmatically affirmative view of different versions of a rational, productivist modernity. Giddens claims that these perspectives repressed the need for a continual dialogue concerning the nature of the good life, and the kinds of ends to which the means of scientific and technological advance can be put.[17] Philosophic conservatism seeks to recover this lost dialogue, by seeking to identify and repair the 'damaged solidarities' of modernity. This approach is indebted to the conservative privileging of local or tacit knowledges in the face of imposing, impersonal philosophical systems and social blueprints. However, the traditional conservative approach tended to favour received tradition and authority symbols as standards against which to judge conduct. By contrast, Giddens draws on his analysis of the 'social revolutions of our time' to suggest that such a standard should be *negotiated*. We have seen that in a reflexive, detraditionalised world, appeals to status and tradition alone are not sustainable. Progressive politics thus becomes an exercise in creating the 'dialogic spaces' in which decisions about social goods and bads can be negotiated. The task of politics is not to impose, top-down, the ready-made truths of left and right. Instead, it is to create the 'dialogic' spaces in which the solutions to problems can be found on a context-dependent basis.[18] This is the essence of the Third Way emphasis upon shifting from the state as provider to the state as *enabler*. As New Labour's then Shadow Chancellor Gordon Brown wrote, shortly after the publication of Giddens' *Beyond Left and Right*, 're-inventing collective action ... requires new thinking about the role of government, not so much as owner or employer, as traditionally conceived, but as partner, enabler, catalyst and co-ordinator.'[19]

This analysis of the left's role echoes Giddens' account of manufactured uncertainty. Our interventions into the social and natural worlds, coupled with increased scepticism about 'experts' and universal solutions, have placed a primacy on the management of risk. Geoff Mulgan, who went on to head the Downing Street Policy Unit, highlights the link between this recognition of doubt and philosophic conservatism:

> By recognising the limits of our knowledge, and by gaining a more sophisticated understanding of change we can draw practical lessons about how policies should be formulated and about how the world can be changed ... For nowadays the left is in many ways most effective when it plays a defensive role, carefully constructing the space for freedom and real life, and protecting people from the dangers of this world rather than promising them a new one.[20]

Philosophic conservatism is thus an attempt give the defensive role for the left a positive connotation that constitutes a form of Third

Way. This involves not clinging on to outdated ideas, nor dogmatically affirming the new times, but rather enabling the protection of valued practices amidst necessary modernisation. Such an ethos is captured in the view of the Third Way's task as being 'to liberate market forces while easing the transition for those who would otherwise fall behind'.[21] It provides a theoretical sketch of a possible role for the centre-left in the face of new times, by recombining aspects of left and right.

The problem for centre-left political strategists is that philosophic conservatism in no sense provides a *programmatic* outline for a centre-left party such as New Labour. Philosophic conservatism is an account of the necessary, defensive function of politics per se, rather than a programme that is *necessarily* of the centre-left. Talk of acting as a facilitator for dialogue is unlikely to appeal to voters used to parties competing on the basis of definite programmes. So for the Third Way – defined as a *recombination* of left and right – to be viable as a political strategy, it needs to show how such recombinations work at the level of political ideologies, parties and programmes. It is on this basis that Third Wayers deploy the use of 'and', reconciling previously opposed elements of left and right in distinctively new combinations. For example, in defining the 'radical centre' of the Third Way, MP Tony Wright suggested that:

> We may talk of synthesis and balance in describing [the radical centre], but the product is something different and distinctive from its parts. Instead of state *or* market (the basis for the post-war mixed economy), the radical centre thinks in terms of state *and* market. It deals similarly with a whole range of other false opposites.[22]

Given these sort of statements, Driver and Martell conclude that 'it is in the combinations that the originality of third way thinking lies. And it is the combination which produces a politics which is both new – "beyond Old Left and New Right" – yet also rooted in Centre-Left values.'[23] The recombination of left and right thus suggests that the categories remain relevant, and that there still exists a space for political agency in the face of rapid social transformations. Philosophic conservatism attempts to give the defensive role of the left a positive dimension, protecting the practices and 'dialogic spaces' that can be undermined by a dogmatic, untrammelled modernisation. Reconciling 'false' opposites, such as state *and* market or fairness *and* efficiency, maintains an affinity with the ethos of preservation underpinning philosophic conservatism. It implies that the Third Way accepts the dynamism of the new times, but that it can simultaneously protect those areas that it values. Thus, economic efficiency is promoted through deregulation and flexible labour markets, but policies are also put in place to combat the market's dislocatory effects. The latter include the minimum wage and programmes aimed at overcoming social exclusion.

Summary

Three interrelated accounts of the effect of social change upon left/right have been identified as informing the Third Way: undermining, reconfiguring and recombining. *Undermining* has occurred through the development of a detraditionalised, reflexive society in which totalising, prescriptive political programmes of left and right are no longer accepted. As the social conditions underpinning traditional versions of left and right have collapsed, what has traditionally been regarded as progressive or conservative has been *reconfigured*. It was the neoliberal right who appeared as the radical force in British politics. The one-nation, paternalist wing of conservatism on the right, and Keynesianism/democratic socialism on the left, appeared to be conservatively defending a vanishing order. For Third Way politics to be of the centre-left, it had to show that like the neoliberals it had embraced the new times, but that it was able to defend and develop the areas of social life that an unchecked neoliberalism threatens. This involved the active recombination of elements of left and right. At a theoretical level, such a response is reflected in the concept of philosophic conservatism, seeking to defend areas of social life in which a dialogue about society's choices can be negotiated. A more political response is evident in Third Way attempts to reconcile philosophical and policy positions that were hitherto more rigidly associated with left and right, e.g. economic efficiency *and* social justice.

In one sense, evident in Giddens' characterisation of the Third Way as the natural accompaniment to a new, reflexive stage of modernity, the Third Way appears as *inevitable*. The rhetorical strength of this is that those who attack the Third Way from either left or right appear to be *irrational*, as standing against the 'real-world' developments that have turned left and right into 'fundamentalisms'. This logic is deployed vividly in Blair's categorisation of both the Conservative Party and the old left as the 'forces of conservatism'.[24] However, for the Third Way to also be the programme of a modernised centre-left, it needs to be shown to be distinct from both Keynesian social democracy (old left) and neoliberalism (New Right). This cannot be achieved by simply pointing to the 'inevitable' outcome of social processes, but necessitates the active *recombination* of left and right. There is thus a tension between versions of the Third Way as a doctrine of sociological inevitability on the one hand, and those that actively introduce a normative, values-based dimension to the project on the other; this tension is pursued throughout the following chapters. But first we turn to the more specific social changes invoked by the Third Way, again assessing how they impact upon left/right.

Social change and Third Way politics

Giddens claims that 'Third way politics, as I conceive of it, is … concerned with restructuring social democratic doctrines to respond to the twin revolutions of globalization and the knowledge economy.'[25] This section examines the role of these specific processes in Third Way theory and politics. A discussion of the role of globalisation is followed by consideration of the effects of new technologies and changes in the nature of work upon political identities. The combined effect of these changes upon the relationship between work, welfare and social exclusion are then outlined. Again, the objective is to identify how Third Wayers invoke social change, and how this relates to claims about the undermining, reconfiguring and recombination of left and right. The overall argument is that the Third Way suggests that the conditions, mechanisms and agents of the Keynesian social democratic settlement have been *undermined*. This leads to a *reconfiguration* in which the parameters of social democracy are altered. Within this new political space, Third Wayers also present neoliberalism as an ultimately failed response to a changed context, and use the *recombination* of left and right to mark out a distinctively Third Way position.

Economic globalisation, left, right and social democracy

Globalisation is, for Giddens, the motor behind individualisation, detraditionalisation and the shift into a new age of reflexive modernity.

It is also the most frequently invoked process in the analysis and rhetoric of Third Way practitioners. As Hay notes, 'the significance of globalisation and claims made about globalisation to the political economy of New Labour can scarcely be overstated'.[26] Challenges to the Third Way's particular mantra of economic globalisation abound. Most fundamentally, some commentators question whether heightened economic globalisation is in fact empirically demonstrable.[27] Others suggest that the role of the nation-state, and the importance of domestic politics as a filter for external influences, have been written off too quickly.[28] There are also different interpretations as to what drives economic globalisation, with important consequences for the political implications that are inferred. Thus, those who are broadly supportive of the global liberalisation of trade, such as Blair and Giddens, tend to identify neutral technological developments as its basis. Critics, however, lean towards explaining globalisation in terms of either the structural dependence of the state upon capital and/or as a result of the restructuring and intensification of capitalist accumulation strategies; such neo-Marxist critiques are explored in Chapter 4.[29] Despite these debates, in order to understand the relationship of the Third Way to globalisation, it *doesn't matter* which account of globalisation is empirically correct. What matters here is the version of economic globalisation that New Labour *chooses* to invoke, and the implications of this for their political strategy.[30]

The Third Way account of economic globalisation is familiar. Owing to the spread of communication technologies and the liberalisation of trade, capital can move instantaneously around the globe, based upon the decisions of investors. The result is that businesses have to compete globally with regard to their technologies, workforce and products. In terms of social democratic politics, Keynesian demand management by an autonomous nation-state becomes untenable. Unable to manage demand through fiscal policy in their own frontiers, governments must instead focus upon creating favourable conditions for businesses to compete in the global marketplace. At the macro level this involves a commitment to 'sound money': managing the public debt and keeping interest rates, corporate taxes and regulations to a minimum. But the focus for government is on the supply side of the economy where the knowledge, skills and flexibility of workers are at a premium. There is thus an active role for government in developing a workforce equipped to meet the requirements of the new, globalised 'knowledge economy'. This means prioritising entry into work and promoting labour market flexibility. As Giddens summarises, 'The aim of macroeconomic policy is to keep inflation low, limit government borrowing, and use active supply-side measures to foster growth and high levels of employment.'[31]

Third Wayers see the 'facts' of economic globalisation as both inevitable and constraining for social democratic politics. Nevertheless, they are explicitly committed to globalisation, pointing to the increases in living standards that free trade can produce. Giddens is clear that 'Economic globalisation, by and large, has been a success. The problem is how to maximize its positive consequences while limiting its less fortunate effects.'[32] The implications of this model of economic globalisation for the categories of left and right are far-reaching, involving elements of undermining, reconfiguring and recombining the left–right axis.

Economic globalisation is held to have *undermined* post-war social democracy by rendering obsolete its key tool – Keynesian demand management. The latter presumed an autonomous nation-state that could use fiscal policy to determine economic outcomes. On this account, social democracy is defined as consisting in the technical *mechanisms* (Keynesian economic instruments) used during its post-war 'golden period'. Given this, by undermining the possibility of Keynesianism, economic globalisation has undermined social democracy itself. As Wickham-Jones observes, 'One interpretation of this approach is that, at an extreme, the end of the social democratic model (and effectively all its variants) has been reached, a historical phenomenon now exhausted and beyond repair.'[33]

If the historical mechanisms of social democracy are exhausted, in order to survive it needs to be redefined in terms of an enduring set of *values* (ends). The means to achieving such ends are seen as secondary, and adaptable to the times. It is this redefinition that constitutes a *reconfiguration* of left and right, by broadening the parameters of what can be labelled as social democratic strategies. These include, for example, the active promotion of flexible, deregulated labour markets or significant reductions in corporation tax as means towards the goal of adapting to the new realities of economic globalisation. From this perspective, the abandonment of Keynesian demand management and corporatism does not represent the collapse or betrayal of social democracy. Rather, new techniques are deployed to pursue social democracy's enduring ends.

The undermining of Keynesian demand management within the confines of the nation-state in turn leads to a wider reconfiguring of left and right. Being forced to separate ends from means, social democrats create a political space in which they are able to countenance policies that would previously have been off-limits. The *recombination* of left and right then flows from the specific choices Third Wayers make in this reconfigured political space. This is evident in the particular strategies Third Wayers adopt in order to differentiate themselves from both the old left and the New Right. By accepting neoliberal assumptions about the global liberalisation of trade, and by promoting flexible labour markets, the Third Way has clearly distinguished itself from the 'first way' of Keynesian social democracy. However, the Third Way also claims to differ from neoliberalism (the 'second way'). In particular, the Third Way challenges neoliberalism's *laissez-faire* ethos of 'letting the market rip' across as many areas of social and economic life as possible. Instead, Third Wayers envisage an active role for government in managing the successful transition to a fully globalised economy, and handling its effects. This involves developing human capital on the supply side in order to equip individuals with the relevant skills for a flexible, knowledge-based economy. As Giddens summarises:

> In the new information economy, human (and social) capital becomes central to economic success. The cultivation of these forms of capital demands extensive social investment – in education, communications and infrastructure. The principle 'wherever possible invest in human capital' applies equally to the welfare state – which needs to be reconstructed as a 'social investment state.'[34]

At the same time, there is a role for the state in providing a (limited) degree of protection from the unwanted consequences of market forces in certain areas. In New Labour's earlier discourse, the NHS had such a status, evidenced in promises that it is 'safe' in New Labour's hands, and risks privatisation under the Conservatives. Of course, the boundaries of which areas of social life should be protected from marketisation are contested, and constitute one of the key battlegrounds on which differing versions of the Third Way are fought. This has been illustrated by battles within New Labour between 'ultra-modernisers' (Blairites) and others (supposedly Brownites) over the meaning and extent of appropriate 'choice' in hospitals and schools, particularly in the run up to the 2005 general election. This clash was anticipated by Giddens when he suggested that, 'There are large areas of public life that should not be commercialized – although having an open public sphere means that where the boundaries should be drawn can be debated.'[35]

Work and identity

Third Wayers hold that economic globalisation has been accompanied by the rise of information technologies and the emergence of a knowledge economy. This has dramatically changed the nature of work itself, with important consequences for the forming of identities and the shape of social democratic strategies. Changes in the nature of production are particularly important in any assessment of social democratic politics, owing to the productivist analysis it shares with Marxism. Within both perspectives, the nature of the production process is central to the form of the state and to political identities and interests. The historical agent of social democratic politics has been a large, relatively homogenous and unionised working class, with the male breadwinner at its core. This was traditionally envisaged as the decisive group in electing Labour governments who, in return, would pursue social democratic policies to improve the material condition of the working-class majority. The effects of new technologies upon the nature of work have undermined this historical agent. There has been a move from heavy manufacturing based, hierarchical 'command and control' systems to diverse, flexible, innovation and market-led production. In the wider literature this is well documented as the shift from Fordist to post-Fordist systems of production.[36] There follow a number of important consequences for social democracy's relationship with its historic agent.

The decline of both heavy manufacturing industry and the homogeneity of the production line have led to a physical fragmentation of the working class; this group is now less easily identifiable as a uniform entity with a shared experience of labour. Given the left's productivist analysis that work is central to political interests and identity, it follows that identities have become as fragmented as the work experience itself. This makes it difficult for any political movement to claim to speak for the shared interests of a working-class majority. Further processes in and outside of work reinforce this tendency. The shift in the workplace towards network forms of organisation, devolved decision-making, differentiation and speciali-sation reflects the wider processes of individualisation and detradi-tionalisation identified by Giddens.[37] Individuals with greater responsibility and autonomy at work are less likely to accept the statist, top-down approach that has characterised the social demo-cratic view of the state. This individualism is accentuated within post-Fordism; consumption becomes the basis of a 'pick and choose' identity that is difficult to permanently co-opt for a political cause. Krieger suggests that New Labour have embraced these various shifts, to the extent that they have actively attempted to break the founda-tional link between work and political identities altogether.[38]

The political effects of alleged changes in the nature of identity formation are evident in the Third Way's psephological analysis, and in particular the thesis of class and partisan dealignment among the electorate. This thesis holds that as a result of the social and eco-nomic changes described throughout this chapter, social class has become a weak indicator of voting preference. In Giddens' words, 'The class relations that used to be so closely bound up with the polit-ical divisions between left and right are disappearing from view.'[39] Indeed, political allegiance *per se* is less fixed and partisan, evidenced in the rise of the 'floating voter'. This trend is embodied in what political scientists describe as the 'new political culture', in which voters tend to combine 'conservative' views on the economy and government 'bureaucracy' with a socially liberal attitude on cultural issues.[40] This understanding of political culture has clearly influenced Giddens' characterisation of a shift from 'emancipatory politics' to 'life politics'.[41] Where the former was concerned with freedom from various forms of social and economic inequality and oppression, the latter is a dialogue about 'how we should respond to a world in which tradition and custom are losing their hold over our lives, and where science and technology have altered much of what used to be "nature" '.[42] The decline of the link between material interests and politics is thus held to necessitate a shift from politics understood as ideology, to being grounded in *values*.[43] Giddens suggests that 'to be on the left is indeed primarily a matter of values. It won't do to define the left in terms of its hostility to markets.'[44] The assumption here is that whereas ideology tends to rely on fixed material interests, values are better able to tap into the newly diverse lifestyle and ethical concerns of the electorate. Third Way psephology concludes that the new breed of voters are rational consumers of political products. The result is a preference for parties that appear as competent on key specific issues such as health or crime, rather than presenting an overarching ideological programme. As Heffernan notes, parties now have to 'compete for votes in a way not dissimilar to a commercial organization operating within the economic marketplace'.[45]

Returning to our analysis of the effects of social change upon left/right, Third Wayers see changes in technology, work and identity formation as *undermining* the historic agent of social democracy – the collectivised working class. Such changes are also held to have undermined the wider possibility of forming ideology-based political strategies. Instead of trying to shape the preferences of the electorate through political leadership, the task is to accommodate them by treating voters as consumers. These changes in the nature of political identity formation *reconfigure* left and right; they again create a new political space, within which Third Wayers can pursue strategies that would have been off-limits to traditional social democrats. We have seen that economic globalisation led to Third Wayers making a firm distinction between means and ends. This reconfigured left and right by redefining the policies that could be enacted towards supposedly left objectives. A similar process occurs with regard to the effect of new political identities. By shifting from an ideological, class-based, materialist politics to one based upon more generic 'values', the scope of policy strategies under headings such as 'opportunity' or 'equal worth' again creates new political spaces for social democrats. The same is true for the shift to a concern with competence over ideological coherence. Most significant is the apparently broad acceptance that market liberalisation can be progressive. This gives modernising social democrats licence to attempt to use market mechanisms *towards* progressive ends.

As in the case of economic globalisation, it is the choices that Third Wayers make within this new political space that constitutes the *recombination* of left and right. Third Wayers accept the neoliberal emphasis upon the efficiency of markets, along with the value placed upon individual choice and autonomy, as these appear to form part of the new political culture. However, Third Wayers simultaneously seek to differentiate themselves from old left and New Right through new combinations. Rhetorically at least, the Third Way's interpretation of the public's desire for individualisation and autonomy is different from that of the neoliberals. Alongside individualism, the significance of *community* is stressed as part of a normative critique of the isolationism and greed that Third Wayers associate with neoliberalism. In addition, the Third Way emphasis is upon equipping individuals to participate in the new knowledge economy, rather than leaving them to 'sink or swim' as they portray neoliberals as doing. This ethos is embodied in one of the Third Way's many 'ands': economic efficiency *and* social justice.

Work, welfare and social exclusion

Globalisation and changes in the technology and organisation of production also affect the Third Way understanding of the relationship between work, welfare and social exclusion. Third Wayers point to the end of the idea of a job for life, the mass movement of women into employment, a simultaneous growth in part-time work and a pervasive sense of insecurity about work contracts. The move to flexible, short-term contracts and the growth in part-time employment has meant that most people can expect to undergo periods when they are out of work, and will often have to retrain to be able to enter new areas of the economy and keep up with technological innovations. The entry of women into the labour market, and the rise in the number of working mothers, also has major implications with regard to family and childcare policies. The significant problem in the transition to this new type of economy is the emergence of a group who are excluded from it in a number of dimensions. The 'socially excluded' tend to be cut off from the various networks, resources and sources of social capital that integrate individuals into mainstream society.[46]

These twin developments – increasing insecurity for those in work, and the multiple forms of exclusion experienced by those outside of it – have recast ideas about the relationship between work and welfare. The severe long-term unemployment that characterised the neoliberal experiment, and the decline of the conditions suitable for Keynesianism more generally, are held to have undermined the possibility of universal benefits. Rather than administering benefits, the task of New Labour's welfare policy is to use work to bring the excluded back into the mainstream.[47] This new work ethic is evidenced in measures such as the New Deal, the Working Families Tax Credit and the minimum wage – all evidence of a strategy designed to be seen to make work pay.

Again, shifts in the structure of work illustrate how social change has *undermined* old left tenets. Demographic changes and the risk of chronic long-term unemployment have rendered impossible the administration of universal benefits. The traditional welfare state proved insufficient to tackle long-term unemployment and, to its critics, encouraged welfare dependency. Globalisation undermined Keynesian demand management, the macroeconomic tool of social democracy. New technologies and changes in the organisation of production undermined social democracy's historic agent – the collectivised working class. We can add to these that the flexibilisation of work, the growth of a group excluded from the knowledge economy and the skills implications of new technologies have undermined the historic tool for social democratic egalitarianism: the entitlements-based welfare state.

In the light of this *undermining* of both the tools and agents of traditional social democracy, New Labour's changed orientation towards the role of the welfare state illustrates how the left-right axis has been *reconfigured* along the lines of 'radicals and conservatives'. It is also illustrative of how Third Wayers have subsequently elected to *recombine* elements of left and right. On the Third Way account, *both* the old social democratic left and neoliberals have become conservative in their attitude towards work and welfare. The old left are presented as an obstacle to a skills-based knowledge economy. They are charged with focusing on the administration of benefits to passive welfare recipients and encouraging dependency. By neglecting supply-side measures for equipping individuals for work, and by not making the requirement to find work the centre of anti-exclusion strategies, the old left are held to have failed the socially excluded. In Gordon Brown's words, the old left have let welfare measures shift from 'being the means to the end of individual emancipation to appearing to be an end in themselves'.[48] Neoliberals, with their desire for a minimal state, are also accused of neglecting the importance of equipping individuals for the new economy. In addition, they fail to recognise the corrosive effects that the rise of social exclusion has upon the wider economy and society. It is important to note that this critique of neoliberalism is not a normative one (based on their punitive attitude towards the excluded), but is made on the grounds of *economic efficiency* and social cohesion. In this recombination of left and right themes, the neoliberal critique of dependency and administering benefits to passive recipients is accepted, but the social democratic concern with social cohesion is maintained. The response is to envisage an *enabling* state that acts as a springboard, launching people back into work and the mainstream, rather than just a safety net. This image has informed Gordon Brown's vision of welfare:

> The emancipation of the individual, to paraphrase an old quotation, comes not from what the state can do for you but what the state can enable you to do for yourself. So, the welfare state must not simply be a safety net, but must offer pathways out of poverty for people trapped on benefit.[49]

This insistence that the welfare state must be a springboard to work and individual opportunity is a Third Way attempt to combine social justice with economic efficiency, rights with responsibilities. Such an approach requires an integrated view of economic and social policy, with the latter no longer being seen as simply managing the failures of the former. Rather, social policy is considered to be integral to *economic* success. The model reflects Giddens' vision of what he calls 'positive' welfare, through which the state is an active facilitator of both the collective negotiation of new risks, and of individual development. Where the Keynesian welfare state may have been appropriate to a more hierarchical and deferential society, the more individualised and detraditionalised world identified by Giddens requires an empowering 'social investment state'.[50] Again, the novelty of the Third Way lies in the *recombination* of elements of left and right, in an attempt to differentiate itself from both.

Summary

I opened this chapter by claiming that the Third Way is essentially a sociological project: it is underpinned by assumptions about the nature of contemporary social change. These range from the macro social theory of Giddens, which characterises a new stage of modernity, to more specific claims about the economy, work, identity and welfare. Such assumptions impact upon the categories of left and

right, which are variously seen to have been undermined, reconfigured and recombined. This model of the relationship between ideas
about social change and the left–right axis is useful, in that it indicates where more or less room for political agency is implied. The
changes which are held to *undermine* left and right imply little room
for political interventions. However, the *reconfiguration* of left and
right opens up spaces for a reinterpretation of what it means to be on
the left, or to be radical. It is within this space that political agency is
given a role, with Third Wayers seeking to *recombine* elements of left
and right, in an attempt to create a new politics. We are thus left with
elements of Third Way theory that relegate the possibilities for political agency, and those which imply a space to actively construct a
new type of politics. The attempt to elaborate the Third Way as a distinctive political project is encapsulated in efforts at developing a set
of Third Way *values*. The following chapter examines the Third Way's
claims to be based upon values, as well as the efforts of commentators
to identify its political character on this basis.

2
Third Way Values

Third Way values?

Ever since the inception of New Labour, Blair and his project have been widely accused of being purely pragmatic and 'not believing in anything'. There is thus no little irony in the fact that, on the issue of Iraq, Blair gave his most forceful demonstration of conviction-based leadership; yet it is this very conviction that may tarnish his legacy forever. As Martin Jacques observes:

> On this Blair abandoned his normal timidity and caution, ignored the focus groups, took on his opponents and argued his case. It is the only occasion that Blair has behaved like Thatcher as a political leader ... His only resort to political boldness, though, could not have been a bigger miscalculation: Iraq will stand as his epitaph.[1]

However, this chapter argues that on the domestic agenda too, New Labour has attempted to elaborate a distinctive set of Third Way values. It is certain that there will be sustained academic argument about the extent to which Blair's Iraq (mis)adventure was a logical extension of, or deviation from, his Third Way normative core. Here the focus is on establishing that such a core does exist, but that attempts to understand the Third Way purely in terms of its values, or as a political philosophy in the traditional sense, are misplaced. Third Way values need to be understood in relation to its sociological claims. The Third Way's sociological impulses and freewheeling approach to established political ideologies has led to claims that it is not an ideas-based project, that it is not a proper political philosophy. To be sure, this sense has been reinforced by criticisms of New Labour's pragmatism and preoccupation with spin. Nonetheless despite, or perhaps as a result of, claims that the Third Way is a value-free zone, a good deal *has* been written about what Third Way values are and should be.[2] Blair and other leading Third Way practitioners occasionally add to the debate with keynote 'vision' speeches, attempting to give normative coherence to the ongoing actions of centre-left governments. A consistent set of themes has emerged, refuting charges of there being no normative core to the Third Way. Shrewder critics have perceived this; former Deputy Labour Leader Roy Hattersley has continually pointed out from his *Guardian* column that the problem is not that Blair has no beliefs – but that they are the *wrong* beliefs for a social democrat worthy of the name.

Giddens has also offered lists of Third Way values, but his project remains essentially sociological rather than an elaboration of a political philosophy.[3] The most quoted statement of Third Way values, which does overlap with that of Giddens, is Blair's short 1998 Fabian pamphlet. Here Blair emphasises what he feels are the enduring values of democratic socialism, which he contrasts with the means to achieve them. Such values are listed as 'equal worth, opportunity for all, responsibility and community'.[4] The latter three of these reflect the original core statement of New Democrat values, prior to Bill Clinton's 1992 presidential race.[5] Significantly, and in contrast to Giddens, both Blair and the New Democrat politicians portray these values as *driving* the Third Way project. In subsequent years, Blair has continued to insist on the value-led nature of the Third Way, observing in 2002 for example that:

> What is vital now is to explain the 'why' of the programme, to describe it not simply point by point but principle by principle. The reason for the changes we are making is not for their own sake but because they are the means to the fairer society, where aspirations and opportunity are open to all, which we believe in. *The programme is not driven by administration but by values.* [emphasis added][6]

The core values consistently deployed by Blair and other Third Wayers are briefly outlined below. This is followed by an overview of the various attempts to infer from such values where New Labour sits on the left–right axis. I argue that, while there are certainly a set of Third Way values that are discernible in New Labour, the Third Way cannot be understood purely in such abstract terms.

Equal worth, community and the individual

Blair opens his account of Third Way values with a restatement of the basic position that 'Social justice must be founded on the equal worth of each individual, whatever their background, capability, creed or race', and uses this to assert a role for governments in ending discrimination and prejudice.[7] In this apparently unremarkable notion there are two significant implications. The first is that equal *worth* does not suggest that we are all, or should be, the same; the Third Way is clearly opposed to any notion of equality of outcome. Blair has suggested that equality of opportunity, as the basis for a meritocratic society, is his goal. He notes that 'we have a long way to go before people are recognised for their abilities'.[8] When pressed on the issue of equality in an interview in 2001, Blair stressed that the important thing was not levelling down or equality of outcome but 'levelling up' by equipping all individuals to fulfil their potential.[9] He later identified the 'opportunity society' as his goal in keynote speeches in 2004.[10]

More radically, equal worth does not even necessarily amount to a call for equality of opportunity. Examining the social policy record of New Labour in government, a number of commentators suggest that equal worth is operationalised as meaning *equal minimum standards for inclusion*. While nobody should be cut-off from the mainstream (the excluded), considerable inequalities of opportunity can remain in terms of, for example, differential access to education. It is noteworthy that Giddens is highly critical of the notion of meritocracy, arguing that the inheritance of material advantages makes it self-negating.[11] This on its own would represent a significant departure from Blair's invocation of meritocracy. However, the minimalist notion of equal worth represents a retreat even from meritocracy, such is the level of inequality of opportunity it tolerates.

A second of the core values identified by Blair is 'community'. This has been taken up by a number of theorists as the key cohering concept of Third Way thought, through which it is hoped that many of the tensions and anomalies surrounding other normative issues will be resolved.[12] As a starting point, Third Way theorists draw on a claim concerning the irreducible nature of the relationship between the individual and his/her community. This is typically associated with the philosopher John MacMurray, who Blair claims has been influential upon his thought.[13] On this view, humans are held not to be isolated individuals, but exist in a mutual web of interdependence. Blair suggests that 'Human nature is cooperative as well as competitive, selfless as well as self-interested; and society could not function if it was otherwise.'[14] While the observation that individuals are embedded in their social context, that 'environment matters', is seemingly a bland one, Crick has pointed out that:

> When Blair talked of 'social-ism' he seemed to be not rejecting the democratic socialist tradition but coming down in favour of that latter side of it. Man is, indeed, a social animal, and to stress this is not entirely banal politically when we have been told, *ipsa dixit*, that there is no such thing as society.[15]

Thus, in the context of a sustained period of neoliberal, anti-collectivist rhetoric, it was politically necessary to make the case for the importance of social relations as opposed to isolated individuals. Consequently, the stressing of the centrality of communal ties became a recurrent thread in New Labour literature from the mid-1990s.[16] The theme persisted, and in his address to the 2000 Labour Party conference Blair offered 'strong communities' or 'no such thing as society' as one of his 'five choices' to the British people, designed to differentiate New Labour from the Conservatives.[17]

In addition to being used to justify a claim about the socially embedded nature of individuals, community serves further functions in the Third Way. Levitas reviews the approaches of three differing communitarian thinkers who have all been associated with the Third Way: Amitai Etzioni, John Gray and John MacMurray. She notes that as well as seeing the Self as socially embedded, all three thinkers believe that economic interdependence is not of itself sufficient to generate solidarity – moral integration is also required; that the community embodies rights, responsibilities and trust; and that these values are supported in actual communities through the application of informal sanctions.[18]

Despite agreement over the broad purposes of community, there are variations in how the concept is deployed and interpreted. Most fundamentally, there is a lack of clarity over the exact scope of the community that is being invoked. At one level, community refers to a concrete and localised set of norms and practices, forming both the physical and moral context in which the Self is grounded. We might think here of a neighbourhood where personal and kinship ties are strong and there is a broad consensus over norms and values. This is often the type of community identified in the work of communitarian writers such as Etzioni. It is also precisely this kind of 'concrete' community that is the focus of much Third Way social policy. This is evident, for example, in initiatives on local regeneration that seek to utilise the knowledge of local actors. The approach is also visible in crime prevention measures that force the criminal to face the moral approbation of the victim or the local community.

In addition to this localised, concrete understanding of community, the Third Way also invokes the term in a more generalised fashion. Here, community is no longer understood as the everyday neighbourhood or milieu but is envisaged as the more abstract 'nation', embodying national collectivity or belonging, instilled with a moral purpose. At the same time, the individuals who inhabit this national unit are invoked as the amorphous 'the people'. Crick laments that, presented in this way, community is evacuated of the concrete, substantive content that he believes gives it meaning:

> too often, when Blair spoke about restoring a spirit of 'community', he linked community to 'society' and to 'nation', as in Clause Four [of the Labour Party constitution] as amended. They are rather big as communities go; in fact they are not communities at all in the pluralist, decentralist and, indeed, sociological senses of that key concept.[19]

These two levels of community each imply a different degree of individual embeddedness within the group; these in turn have different implications as to what extent and how individual behaviour can be determined. The difference between the two conceptions is again summarised by Crick:

> The sense of solidarity that a whole nation or society can feel is a different thing from the 'community feeling' of a group small

enough to maintain an informal, traditional or voluntary moral order, as distinguished from 'society', which may or may not have a moral consensus, but needs central and general legal restraints and procedural consensus to maintain order.[20]

In the localised understanding of community, behaviour is policed with reference to localised, implicit norms and practices and often informal sanctions. By contrast, in the extended version, the parameters of conduct are generalised and politically defined at the level of the state on behalf of 'the people'. Critics point to how both of these senses of community can drift into authoritarianism. In the case of the localised community, the non-negotiated and potentially arbitrary character of localised norms and practices, coupled with their all-encompassing proximity to the individual, could result in the stifling of individuality. These are charges typically levelled at Etzioni who, Collins notes, 'is often criticized for being, by turns, authoritarian, repressive, atavistic, moralistic'.[21] It is for this reason that Giddens explicitly rejects what he sees as communitarianism's desire for a return to localised community rules. This, he argues, can lead to a divisive 'identity politics' which:

> tends to be exclusivist, and difficult to reconcile with the principles of tolerance and diversity upon which an effective civil society depends. Hence it is to civil society more generally, rather than to 'the community', that we should turn as an essential element of third way politics.[22]

However, others argue that relying on a generalised sense of norms at the level of 'the people' runs the risk of the state crowding out the civil society that Giddens appeals to. The danger here is of the state acting as moral arbiter, defining the content of generalised norms. This bypasses the *intermediary* associations between the individual and the state, usually understood as civil society. Indeed, both the Conservatives and Liberal Democrats have taken opportunities to criticise New Labour's centralising and 'over-regulatory' tendencies in this vein. The content of the norms of the generalised community can all too easily become a reactionary form of populism, through which particular interests are falsely presented as being those of the universal 'nation' or 'people'.[23]

Opportunities, rights and responsibilities

Despite criticisms of community, for Third Wayers its key function is to both provide opportunities and encourage the acceptance of responsibilities. The Third Way sees an active role for government in the creation of substantive, as opposed to just legalistic, opportunity. As White suggests, 'it involves a commitment to substantive or real opportunity for basic goods such as education, jobs, income, and wealth. The notion of a "stakeholder society" can be readily understood as a society which guarantees all citizens at least some level of real opportunity for these basic goods.'[24] Blair endorses this notion of positive freedom (freedom to), as opposed to the negative view of liberty (freedom from) advocated by neoliberalism. However, as was noted above, he and other Third Wayers are also firmly against what they perceive as the levelling-down effect of pursuing equality of outcome. Blair criticises the old left that, 'at worst ... has stifled opportunity in the name of abstract equality.'[25] In practice the Third Way understanding of providing opportunity (as realising equal worth) involves meeting minimum standards of inclusion.

The mantra of 'no rights without responsibilities' is perhaps the most closely associated with New Labour and the Third Way. Advocates suggest that the innovation of the Third Way is to recognise the *reciprocity* of rights and duties. Blair is clear that he is making a *value-judgement* about the old left and New Right for their failure to narrate the importance of responsibility to the community. In the case of the left this amounted to the granting of rights (in the form of welfare benefits in particular), without an emphasis on the reciprocal role of obligations. Such criticism came to a controversial head in Blair's 2004 attack on the 1960s 'liberal consensus' which, he claimed, had encouraged 'freedom without responsibility'.[26] For the right, the fault was to define personal responsibility as purely self-interest.[27] Blair seeks to overcome this moral absence by using a communitarian position that locates individual freedoms firmly within the context of responsibilities to the wider community. As he suggests, 'The rights we enjoy reflect the duties we owe: rights and opportunity without responsibility are engines of selfishness and greed.'[28]

Giddens is similarly explicit about the centrality of rights and responsibilities to his conception of the Third Way:

> Having abandoned collectivism, third way politics looks for a new relationship between the individual and the community, a

redefinition of rights and obligations. One might suggest as a prime motto for the new politics, *no rights without responsibilities* ... Old style social democracy ... was inclined to treat rights as unconditional claims. With expanding individualism should come an extension of individual obligations.[29]

While government has a role to play in the creation of opportunities, citizens must accept their responsibilities to, for example, seek work in return for benefits or fulfil their duties as parents. The interdependence of Third Way values is evident in that it is at the level of the community that this synthesis of rights and responsibilities is to be realised.

Accountability, transparency and devolution

A final group of Third Way 'values' concerns transparency, accountability, and devolution in politics and public life.[30] The ethos of rights matching responsibilities necessitates transparency in mapping out exactly what can be expected of government and citizens alike. This thinking is evident in the numerous contracts that abound in Third Way policy-making, such as the requirements placed upon jobseekers in return for benefits, or home–school contracts between schools, pupils and their parents. If rights and responsibilities are to be enforced, the relevant parties need to be held accountable in the event of a breakdown of the contract.

An emphasis on transparency and devolution is also appropriate to the Third Way's sociological analysis of a detraditionalised and individualised society. It was shown in Chapter 1 how Giddens identifies the collapse of hierarchical, command and control forms of governance under these twin pressures. On this basis he calls for a 'dialogic' reasoning in which decisions must be justified transparently and through an inclusive, rational dialogue.[31] Subsidiarity – the devolution of decision-making to the most local level possible – is thus identified by Third Wayers as the best means of adapting political decision-making to social realities. In policy terms New Labour's devolutionary measures – including national and regional assemblies and developments such as increased use of referenda and City Mayors – can be seen as gesturing towards this requirement. An ethos of participation and transparency is also evident in citizens' panels, community-led regeneration schemes and the proliferation of various means of auditing in the name of public accountability. While the limitations of these devices as deployed by New Labour have been severely criticised, they nevertheless reflect Third Way preoccupations with modernising decision-making mechanisms to better reflect a changed social context.

Summary

Following Blair's original 1998 pamphlet, there has been a good deal of agreement among Third Way practitioners and commentators over what constitutes Third Way values. However, this is not to say that there is not considerable room for disagreement over how such values are to be interpreted and operationalised.[32] 'Equal worth' serves the useful political function for modernisers of appealing to egalitarian instincts, while simultaneously backtracking from commitments to equality of outcome. It has even enabled a retreat from equality of opportunity, to a position of providing minimum standards for inclusion. The Third Way outlines a reciprocal relationship between the individual and community. This also serves a political function, of recognising the importance of individuals (vital, given the increasingly individualist aspirations of the electorate), while differentiating the Third Way from the 'no such thing as society' stance of neoliberalism. However, community also acts as the site where the values of opportunity, rights and responsibilities take shape. The community is identified as the source of (a minimum level of) opportunities and rights. At the same time, it is in the name of community that the various responsibilities of citizens are invoked. Finally, for an ethos of rights and responsibilities to be effectively realised, there needs to be greater transparency, accountability and devolution in the political process. These characteristics are also appropriate to the Third Way's sociological account of growing individualisation and the decline of traditional modes of authority.

Using values to locate the Third Way

Much – perhaps too much – of the academic debate over New Labour and the Third Way has concerned definitions. In particular, commentators have pondered what the broad Third Way values discussed above reveal about its relationship to the categories of left and right. Protagonists in such debates tend to see Third Way values as being variously: of the right in the form of a capitulation to neoliberalism;

as combining elements of left and right; or as being on the left and remaining true to a social democratic tradition. These arguments are summarised below, where it is argued that analyses of values on a pre-given, static left–right axis, fail to capture the genesis of the Third Way. The values of the Third Way need to be considered in *relation to* its sociological claims, and this will be the task of Chapter 3.

The Third Way to the right: neoliberalism

The charge that the Third Way has adopted the values of the neoliberal right is commonplace, with a number of areas pointed to as evidence. Firstly, where the old left, in its various forms, held in common an ethical as well as an economic critique of capitalism, the Third Way has abandoned even the pretence of such a position. As Crouch notes:

> Inter-war Labour had said: 'Nothing can be done about the markets (yet); we must just try to protect our people from their ravages.' New Labour says: 'Nothing can be done about the markets (ever); we must help our people adapt to their requirements.'[33]

Markets, and the subsequent enormous wealth that a minority of entrepreneurs are able to accrue, are not only accepted but positively *celebrated* by advocates of the Third Way. Indeed, Peter Mandelson famously noted that New Labour 'is intensely relaxed about people getting filthy rich'.[34] Allen observes of this tendency that:

> Third Way theorists rarely engage in a discussion of business except by way of a celebration of the innovation, mutability and efficiency purportedly characteristic of private enterprise, in contrast to the conservatism, stasis and under-performance of the state.[35]

On this view, Third Way values are in fact a reflection of this capitulation to the requirements of the free market. In particular, they are a conduit for the retrenchment of the welfare state. Thus, the notion of equal worth, defined as minimum standards of inclusion, signifies a retreat from a commitment to reducing inequality of outcome through redistribution. The celebration of wealth-creating entrepreneurs is a basis for avoiding high marginal rates of tax, which are held to act as a disincentive to such wealth generation. It also justifies deregulation in the name of creating labour-market 'flexibility', which Fairclough suggests is 'a word that tends to stand for the whole neo-liberal project'.[36] Similarly, the rhetoric of 'no rights without responsibilities', embodied in welfare-to-work programmes, reflects a shift from comprehensive social protection to placing the onus to find work upon the individual. While the right to generate profit is taken as given, the responsibilities of the super-rich to pay taxes, or those of employers towards their employees, are not highlighted with the same fervour. Interestingly, work by Burnham implies that even the Third Way values of transparency, accountability and devo- lution of powers in economic and other policy decision-making, can be accounted for in terms of the state's relationship to capital. With this 'depoliticising' strategy, the state attempts to gain credibility with capital by appearing to be 'once removed' from economic deci- sion-making. The vehicle for this is a shift towards rules-based, as opposed to discretion-based, economic management.[37]

In addition to sharing neoliberalism's celebration of capitalism, the Third Way is also criticised for echoing its conservative and authori- tarian cultural elements. At its most extreme, this is held to reflect the 'authoritarian populism' identified by Stuart Hall in the discourse of Thatcherism during the 1980s.[38] On this view, rather than being seen as a site of empowerment for the individual, community comes to represent the imposition of enforced, typically conservative, norms and values (see Chapter 8). This links again with responsibility, in particular with the prescriptive attitude taken towards responsibilities to seek work, and also in criminal justice measures. Levitas has iden- tified a 'moral underclass discourse' underpinning New Labour wel- fare and criminal justice policies, which assumes individualistic, cultural explanations of poverty. This is in tension with discourses of redistribution, associated with the old left, or of inclusion, associated with stakeholding.[39] Finally, in order to execute their economic and cultural project, like the neoliberals, Third Way politicians (despite devolutionary measures) rely on a strong state with a dominant core executive. Taken together, accounts which identify the Third Way as an extension of neoliberalism see it as continuing in the framework of the 'free economy and the strong state', famously identified by Andrew Gamble as characterising Thatcherism.[40]

The Third Way as combination of left and right

Driver and Martell suggest that the Third Way is defined not just in opposition to the old left or New Right, but tries to combine them in positive ways. In so doing, Third Wayers may produce configurations that are neither left nor right.[41] The themes of community, and rights and responsibilities, can be seen to draw on old left (and traditional conservative) concerns with social cohesion, as well as a liberal contractual emphasis on self-help and the fulfilling of obligations. This theme is developed by Freeden, who locates New Labour between liberalism, conservatism and socialism without being equidistant from each of them. From liberalism, there is a concern with individual choice and responsibility; from conservatism, a stress on productivity, shared norms and duties, strong leadership and an attachment to lost values; finally, the socialist element is represented in the affirmation of the existence of society and the centrality of community.[42]

Others suggest that the Third Way is given coherence through its very eclecticism, which brings it close to the New Liberalism of the early twentieth century.[43] Vincent argues that debates about the Third Way, or 'New Socialism', represent the elements which constituted the New Liberalism after 1914. While there is debate concerning the extent to which figures such as T.H. Green, J.A. Hobson, L.T. Hobhouse and later Beveridge and Keynes were 'New Liberals', pre-1914 New Liberalism can be characterised as reacting against the atomised, *laissez-faire* approach of classical or 'old' liberalism. Instead it sought:

> a more socialised and holistic understanding of the individual, a more positive conception of liberty linked to notions like self-development, a modified conception of a market economy and a more responsive, sensitive and ethical conception of the state.[44]

Vincent suggests that after 1914, this New Liberalism itself developed left, centre and right variations which have characterised the major forms of left thinking in Britain in the twentieth century. He argues that contemporary ideological competition, between the neoliberal right and the Third Way of the centre-left, mirrors the struggle between 'classical' and 'new' liberalism. Post-war Keynesian social democracy was the most notable New Liberal achievement, old liberalism made a return through the neoliberal right in the 1980s, and now the Third Way has again brought New Liberal concerns to the fore.

> What is called New Labour is a redrafting of components of the new liberalism which has, in fact, recovered some of the pre-1914

'new liberal' language ... therefore, neither New Right nor New Labour is really new, rather, a fecund liberal vocabulary has been reinterpreted by both.[45]

The Third Way to the left: social democratic revisionism

Finally in this typology are those who locate the Third Way in the tradition of social democratic revisionism. On this view, Third Way values are the latest attempt to adapt social democratic means to the enduring goal of simply managing capitalism.[46] As Rubinstein observes:

> The Labour Party has in reality never attempted to do more than ameliorate the worst excesses of capitalist society. It is trying to do so still, sobered by the understanding that Thatcherite Conservatism found a real echo in the minds of the British people.[47]

Analysis of this sort points to the emphasis on work and productivity, centralising instincts and cultural conservatism of previous social democratic governments, and suggests that the Third Way is but the latest manifestation of these tendencies. On this view, even the centrality of 'opportunity' to Third Way values is in keeping with Labour's traditions. For Rubinstein, 'The policy of the Labour Party is as it has been – one that seeks to increase individual rights and opportunities.'[48]

Others suggest that the focus of social scientists on the present and future leads to a desire to demonstrate that New Labour represents a radical break with Labour's past.[49] This, of course, is also precisely the objective of the New Labour leadership in trying to distance itself from a homogenised 'old left'. The result is to gloss over the historical evidence which reveals a remarkable degree of consistency between the broad objectives of 'old' and 'new' Labour. Bale points to a tendency to forget that the:

> frequency with which the party leadership in government sought to remind supporters and electors that welfare would require 'tough choices', 'thinking the unthinkable' and 'compassion with a hard edge' was par for the course by 1968, let alone 1998.[50]

For those who see continuity in the Third Way, then, it is the latest version (for better or worse!) of a social democratic revisionism that must, by definition, continually adapt its means as the society it seeks to manage develops. Social democratic responses to the Third Way are analysed in detail in Chapter 6.

Assessment: the limits of normative approaches

Although there is a degree of consensus among Third Wayers over their stated values, there have nevertheless been ongoing calls for the development of a clearer, bolder set of principles to guide the project. However, repeated relaunches – and announcements that New Labour has finally discovered what it believes in – only provoke cynicism the longer that it is in office. Numerous lists of values, and various attempts to define in *a priori* terms what is meant by equal worth or community, have an arbitrary, 'back of an envelope' feel. Consequently, charges of the empty use of slogans have been persistently made against New Labour and Third Way rhetoric. This is particularly the case with the range of secondary concepts that are often used as the means to achieving normative ends. These include 'partnership', 'modernisation' and, during the 2001 and 2005 general election campaigns, 'aspiration'. Used in a vacuum, these terms can be deployed with such rhetorical flexibility as to be devoid of substantive meaning.[51] By 2004, the Conservatives saw this tendency as an opportunity to attack Labour's attempts to develop a big idea for a third term. Party Chairman Liam Fox said of Blair's call for an 'opportunity society':

> He cannot stop talking about building new societies and new economies. So far we've had 'the decent society', the 'creative economy', 'a stakeholder economy', 'a new Age of Achievement' and 'the partnership economy'. Not to mention 'New Labour's Millennium Challenge', 'the information superhighway', 'a people's Europe' and, of course, 'the third way'.[52]

But by defining the Third Way purely in terms of values (or an absence of them), critics face similar problems to Third Wayers themselves. Tending to work with static notions of left and right, and their concomitant ideologies, 'value-centric' appraisals of the Third Way face three problems. First, they rely on the same *a priori* categories as value-based articulations of the Third Way. These categories have sustained debates concerning, for example, the nature of liberalism and socialism and the relations between them, regardless of changing historical circumstances. An all too familiar set of arguments is reproduced *ad infinitum*. This is not to say that debates about the character of the Third Way in relation to, say, New Liberalism are unimportant or cannot produce any insights, but they are not sensitive to the specific empirical dynamics that gave rise to the Third Way. Such debates are ill-equipped to scrutinise claims to the *novelty* of Third Way politics in the light of sociological developments of the sort outlined in Chapter 1. Given the Third Way's claims that the categories of left and right have been radically altered, and that it represents a departure from them, attempting to evaluate the Third Way against a static and enduring left–right axis is self-evidently problematic. In addition, attempts to compare the Third Way to previous ideological projects neglects those projects' fluidity and diversity. There is no uniform benchmark of traditional social democracy, for example, against which to compare the Third Way (of which more in Chapter 6).[53] Ironically, to posit a homogenous 'old-style' social democracy, as a means of criticising the Third Way, in fact *reproduces* the Third Way's own conflation of diverse left traditions as simply a redundant 'old left'.

A second difficulty with value-centric perspectives is the sense that those placing the Third Way on a static left–right axis simply project their own normative aspirations into their analysis. This has the potential to occur in all social science and, particularly given the parameters of this study, I am certainly not advocating the desirability or possibility of absolute value-freedom. However, the use of static, pre-given categories exacerbates this potential problem. Having adopted a fixed model of what constitutes 'neoliberalism', 'social democracy' or 'New Liberalism', critics then simply attempt to make Third Way ideas or programmes fit the particular ideal-type. Alternatively, any departure from the ideal-type by the actually existing Third Way can be labelled a betrayal.[54] Any prejudicial desire to criticise the Third Way for being neoliberal, or to defend it as in the tradition of social democracy, is magnified by the use of static left/right categories.

The above two problems result in a third, more fundamental one. By reproducing long-standing debates over left and right, and by trying to make Third Way politics fit pre-existing models, value-centric approaches to the Third Way seldom move beyond the level of *description*. This is perhaps surprising, given that those calling for the Third Way to adopt an alternative set of values have a *critical* yardstick against which they can judge its deficiencies, for example with regard to the principle of equality. However, a good deal of value-based analysis of the Third Way concentrates on what it 'is' in terms of enduring ideological positions. There is a failure to engage with the Third Way's sociological components, preferring instead pre-existing normative debates. This results in an ideo-centric account of the Third Way's origins, and an insufficient basis from which to map its possible *futures*. The sociological basis of the Third Way must be examined to understand its origins, content and possible trajectory.

In sum, both discussions of individual Third Way values, and attempts to locate them in terms of enduring debates over left and right ideologies, fail to provide an adequate account of Third Way politics or its possible futures. Focusing purely on the Third Way's normative components fails to address the questions of why Third Way ideas emerged at this particular historical conjuncture, what processes and constituencies underpin them, and, vitally, how they might come to be contested. Attempts to tag a set of principles onto a governing project misunderstand how successful political strategies are developed. The analytical task is to theorise the *relationship between* the Third Way's sociological and normative claims. This is the objective of Chapter 3.

3
Analysing Social Change and Political Strategy

So far we have seen that the Third Way is driven by sociological imperatives, as a response to a 'changed world', but that Third Wayers have also sought a distinctive set of values to frame their project. Given this, we need to understand the relationship between these twin tracks: what opportunities does social change present for political interventions? New Labour has been continually criticised for failing to communicate an overarching political narrative or 'story' to the electorate, as Thatcherism was able to. Enduring political projects, as Mrs Thatcher and her strategists knew, are able to win the 'battle of hearts and minds' and create a shift in the political culture. This is achieved by identifying the key elements of social change, and then allying them to a set of values in order to steer society in a definite political direction. The art of politics is this mediation between macro social changes and normative political values. Thus, the Thatcherites identified the aspiration that went along with what sociologists label increasing individualisation. They successfully linked this to a neoliberal discourse of 'freedom' and 'opportunity', which they contrasted to the stifling collectivism of the left.[1]

The following account of the Third Way's understanding of the relations between social change and political values shows why it has been unable to develop a similarly resonant narrative of its own; one that is both grounded in social change, but also shows how a distinctive political project can steer it. Four different types of claim concerning the nature of this relationship can be discerned in the Third Way: none are exclusively associated with a particular theorist or advocate, and the same individuals often implicitly make more than one type of claim. Each type implies a different interpretation of the space for political agency to shape the content of centre-left politics, and the social forces that underpin it. These range from a position which subordinates politics to the imperatives of social change, to one which emphasises the role of values and political leadership.

Sociological-value relations in the Third Way

1 Values as a functional response to social change

At its most deterministic, Third Way sociological analysis sees values as subordinate to the imperatives of social change. In their joint statement on the Third Way, Blair and SPD German Chancellor Schroeder suggest that, 'Modernization is about adapting to conditions that have objectively changed.'[2] Rather than trying to give the Third Way a normative content, this approach sees values as a *functional* response to the kinds of social processes identified in Chapter 1. This position reflects Giddens' sociology of the decline of left and right, which attempts to match values to a prior sociological analysis.[3] Giddens is not interested in combining the values of old left or New Right to produce a new political philosophy. Instead, he highlights social processes such as globalisation and detraditionalisation and develops Third Way 'values' as a response to them.[4] For example, Giddens tends not to launch a *moral* critique of either the statism of the old left or the possessive individualism of the New Right, as Blair might. Giddens claims that the statism of the old left is redundant not because of a normative failure, such as neglecting individual responsibility or aspiration. Rather, socialism collapsed, most spectacularly in the USSR, because of the emergence of a globalised, detraditionalised and reflexive world in which 'providential' views of historical progress and statist, top-down command systems (such as the communist polity and economy) were no longer viable.[5] For Giddens, Third Way values need to be developed as a response to these major shifts. For example, like Blair, Giddens sees 'no rights without responsibilities' as a potential motto for Third Way politics.[6] However, where Blair bases this position on a claim about the irreducible relationship between the individual and the community, for Giddens it is *after the fact* of the social process of individualisation that obligations must be emphasised. He notes that, 'Old style social democracy ... was inclined to treat rights as unconditional claims.

With expanding individualism should come an extension of individual obligations' (emphasis added).[7]

For Giddens, then, the values of the Third Way are a *post facto*, functional response to the 'social revolutions of our time', not to be understood on an *a priori* basis as being valuable in themselves. He suggests that, 'The overall aim of third way politics should be to help citizens pilot their way through the major revolutions of our time: *globalization, transformations in personal life* and our *relationship to nature.*'[8] This approach reflects Giddens' grounding in the sociological tradition. It takes as its starting point social processes that occur above the intentions and actions of individuals, and sees its task as creating a form of politics that is appropriate to them. It is a *technocratic* position, as once the core social processes have been identified, the appropriate political responses are held to be self-evident. This mindset is revealed where Third Wayers dismiss – as obsolete – political responses that are apparently not based on the relevant sociological analysis (e.g. as the 'forces of conservatism'). In this functionalist analysis, there is little room for either ideological disagreement based upon normative differences, or for political leadership and conviction politics of the kind that might try to *shape* a particular version of the good society. If this approach is adopted by politicians, the notion of the 'end of ideology' becomes self-fulfilling: political programmes are formed on the basis of technocratic responses to social processes that are treated as givens.

2 Updating values

A second approach suggests that old values must be *updated* to meet changed circumstances. For example, Blair claims in his 1998 pamphlet that the Third Way 'is about traditional values in a changed world'.[9] This is similar to the functional approach in that it takes as given certain 'facts' about the new social terrain, from which different values must follow. However, in the functional response, the values themselves are *derived* from the sociology. New concepts, with apparently no grounding in any ideological tradition, are designed to 'fit' the new society. Alternatively, in the updating approach, the values appropriate to new times are grounded in an enduring normative tradition. The ethos that guides the values remains constant, but their expression must take into account the new times. This approach is commonly found in the discourse of centre-left party modernisers.

It can reassure traditional supporters that the core values of the party are being preserved, while simultaneously introducing significant policy shifts. The updating values approach was thus integral to justifying the 'modernisation' of the Labour Party into New Labour. Pierson notes that Labour's influential Commission on Social Justice (CSJ) report of 1994 'was self-consciously presented as a renovation of social democratic principles under changing circumstances rather than as the attempt to forge an alternative'.[10] In the same year, the updating approach was explicitly adopted by emerging New Labour figures. In the introduction to an influential collection of essays, David Miliband argued for 'the politics of a constant and continuing reapplication of a set of values to changing circumstance'.[11] Gordon Brown, then Shadow Chancellor, proposed in the same volume that, 'To modernize our policies – like our organization – is not to change or dilute our values: it is instead to revive them and make them relevant for these new challenges.'[12] Over a decade on from these debates framing the transition to New Labour, the updating values approach remains a key tool for modernisers. Praising the success of the New Labour ethos of 'traditional values in a modern setting', Blair told his National Policy Forum in 2004 that:

> By reconnecting with our historic values and applying them to the modern world we have reclaimed for our movement the idea that rights should be matched by responsibilities, that individual aspiration can and must be allied with social solidarity. Steadfast in our values, radical in our means, that is the New Labour way.[13]

Modernisers can demonstrate to target voters that they are in step with new times, while presenting policy changes in a language of continuity that keeps core supporters on board.

3 A historical confluence between values and circumstance

A third type of claim also identifies the sweeping significance of new times. However, it does not suggest that new values need to be developed as a functional response to social change, or that enduring values need updating. Instead, this approach argues that the values remain the same and have been given a new relevance precisely because of the nature of social change. There is thus a *historical confluence* between a set of enduring social democratic values, and the contemporary circumstances that such values are best equipped to address. Illustrating how the same individual can make more than one of the types of claim identified here, in the same piece cited above in which Gordon Brown adopts the updating values approach he also suggests that 'socialist theory fits the economic facts of the 1990s more closely than those of the 1890s'.[14] It is not that values need updating, but that they have been made particularly relevant by contemporary economic and social conditions.

The most typical example of the historical confluence position is the tactic of appealing to business to accept centre-left proposals on the grounds that they are, in fact, *efficient*.[15] Low wages, inequality, poor working conditions and other traditional left issues are not cited as problems on moral or political grounds. Instead it is argued that, in the modern global economy, such problems hamper efficient business practice, productivity and growth. A stark example is provided in a contribution by Kapstein to a collection of Third Way writings. He suggests, apparently without irony, that with regard to the developing world, 'it is hard to develop an economy when large numbers of workers are dying in what should be the prime of life'.[16]

Kapstein argues that this fact should be used to highlight the value of universal healthcare. Similarly, environmental degradation should be avoided as those whose health it destroys are 'less capable of realizing their talents. The result is a waste of human resources.'[17] No matter the ethical rights or wrongs of pollution and high mortality rates, the fact is that they impede workers from reaching full productivity. As Blair put it in his Leader's Speech of 2000, 'What began as a moral crusade is now also the path to prosperity. What started as a belief in the equal worth of all is also a programme for wealth creation.'[18] In 2004 Gordon Brown deployed exactly the same tactic by claiming 'the countries that will succeed best in the global economy will be those that bring out the best talents of all no matter their birth race, sex or background'.[19] Social justice and economic productivity are presented as enhancing one another.

The historical confluence approach is, strategically, the riskiest of the four identified here. Rhetorically, it has the advantage of placing Third Way values and policies at the centre of contemporary events, as being with the spirit of the times. However, if the Third Way is tied to a set of historically contingent circumstances, a radical change in those circumstances would make the values obsolete. If Third Way advocates recognise that history is open-ended, then they must acknowledge that the alleged coincidence of business interests with progressive reforms is itself not necessarily permanent. In rougher economic times, business may well conclude that efficiency and profitability can only be restored through traditional means: downsizing, minimising investment and calling for cuts in public expenditure. Progressive measures may then well be discarded, along with the life-chances of those they sought to protect. This problem can only be solved by the theoretical belief that present circumstances (e.g. globalisation, the knowledge economy) are permanent, representing the 'end of history'. However, this would involve precisely the kind of teleological, 'providential' view of history that Giddens and other Third Way thinkers criticise in the old left.[20] At its most extreme, the historical confluence perspective leads to the most overblown statements, suggesting that the Third Way does represent some kind of historical endgame. Blair was adopting the historical confluence approach on telling his party conference:

> Today a strong economy and a strong society are sides of the same coin ... self interest and the common good at last in harmony ... Realism and idealism at long last in harmony.[21]

4 The Third Way as value-led

The final position in this typology, permitting the greatest scope for political agency, stresses the role of values in forming political strategies. The specific value-led elements of the Third Way, and the problems of characterising it in such terms, were detailed in Chapter 2. From the value-led perspective, social change is seen as open-ended and always subject to political intervention. Factual conditions are never neutral, but always the result of previous, value-driven political decisions or struggles. On this basis, it is the importance of *political leadership* that is emphasised, in terms of both steering social change and creating the climate for such changes to be interpreted through particular values. In particular, New Labour modernisers were acutely aware of the role that a guiding set of values played in the electoral success of Thatcherism, despite being critical of their content. Commenting on the Conservative legacy of 'boom and bust', Gordon

Brown argued that 'These things didn't just happen – the flawed values of the Tory Party made them happen.'[22]

Third Wayers frequently claim that their project should be driven by the 'right' values. Blair has been particularly keen to stress that the Third Way is a value-driven project, famously replying to those who thought that with a second term in office he would jettison the façade of New Labour, 'It's worse than you think: I really do believe in it.'[23] The desire to present the Third Way as value-led can translate into an almost evangelical zeal, evidenced in the claim of Australian Labour politician Mark Latham that:

> Common values help glue society together. They give us a collective sense of purpose and normality.[...] *This is why the third way sees politics as an exercise in conviction and the teaching of values.* [...] It denotes a renaissance in the moral foundations of socialism. [emphasis added][24]

In this vein, Gordon Brown made value-based leadership the central theme of his 2004 Labour Conference speech, in which he called for the delivery of a 'progressive consensus':

> Our task therefore is not to consolidate the politics we inherited but by our words and deeds to transform people's view of what in our country is possible ... Instead of retreating to being administrators for our policies we must also become evangelists for them.[25]

Interestingly, a preference for value-led politics often underpins the severest *criticisms* of the Third Way in general, and New Labour in particular. This is unsurprising, given that the value-led perspective presupposes political *choice*, and as such can always point to alternative possibilities. Media commentators have consistently called upon New Labour to define what its project 'stands for'. They suggest that without a clear statement of principles, the Third Way will fail to entrench long-term support among the electorate and change the political culture in the way that Thatcherism was able to. This theme underpinned the disappointment of many commentators on the tenth anniversary of Blair's leadership of New Labour. Polly Toynbee lamented that:

> All these years in power and a Labour government is still behaving like insurgents into a Tory Britain, as if no progress has been won

since 1994 ... [Blair's] social democratic deeds are mostly done sotto voce without explaining or persuading as he goes.[26]

Jonathan Freedland went further, suggesting that:

> the prime minister has looked for a long time like a man who has run out of ideas. He is not able to sketch a clear picture of the kind of country Britain should become, nor even to set out a few core principles by which all political choices should be decided.[27]

Such critics argue that the absence of a value-led narrative will result in a crisis when the Third Way has to handle political conflict, or face down opponents. The project will have failed to define 'friends and enemies', or develop a stock of principles to refer to when the political going gets tough and hard choices have to be explained to a sceptical public.

These calls for value-based leadership are mirrored in academic analyses which deconstruct claims to the inevitability of Third Way policies. Such work seeks to show how the social processes outlined in Chapter 1, often invoked as external constraints by Third Wayers, are in fact the outcome of definite political choices. Globalisation is the classic example, with Colin Hay commenting with regard to New Labour's claims:

> in so far as globalisation exists, its origins can be traced to a series of highly political (and hence contingent) decisions to deregulate the financial markets and to liberalise capital flows[28]

The implication is that it is ideologically motivated political choices which can ultimately structure social outcomes – different values could result in a different sociological direction. Thus, Hay concludes with an appeal to political leadership, arguing:

> If Labour in office is to impose a new trajectory upon the institutions, processes and practices of the British economy and polity, then it must first win the battle to define and project a new economic paradigm – *a battle for hearts and minds.* [emphasis added][29]

Conclusion: social change, values and political agency in the Third Way

Chapter 1 suggested that the Third Way is underpinned by a sociological analysis. This has fundamental consequences for the categories of left and right, and defines the space for political action. Chapter 2 showed that, alongside this sociological analysis, there is a set of core values in Third Way discourse; commentators typically understand Third Way values in relation to a supposedly enduring left–right axis of political ideologies. Such approaches were criticised for leading to an ideo-centric analysis; this neglects the sociological context identified in Chapter 1, and that Third Wayers themselves see as being central to their project.

This chapter has been premised on the view that to understand the origins, content and possible alternatives to the Third Way, its values need to be understood in *relation* to its sociological analysis. Four variants of this relationship were outlined as existing in Third Way discourse, with more than one type of claim often made by the same individual, or even in the same text. The functional perspective grants the least room for creative political agency; what Giddens refers to as 'the social revolutions of our time' are treated as a *fait accompli* – values simply need to 'fit' to them. Then there are two middling positions with regard to the scope for politics, envisaging a role for enduring social democratic values. The first suggests that it is the means which need updating to meet enduring ends, in order to adapt to new circumstances; the second that there is a historical match between contemporary conditions and enduring values. Finally, the position which allows the greatest room for political leadership ascribes primacy to values in shaping social change. I want to argue that, on their own, none of these positions provides a sound strategic basis for the Third Way – or any possible reconstruction.

Most obviously, the first position, which sees Third Way values as merely a functional response to social change, is insufficient because it rules out politics from the outset. Politics itself is reduced to the technocratic search for values that fit the pre-given social terrain. This neglects both the constitutive role of political agency in creating that terrain *in the first instance*, and that its future direction can be contested and steered. Giddens himself has come to identify the problems of this approach. His earlier analyses in *Beyond Left and*

Right (1994) and *The Third Way* (1998) argued that social change has undermined the very categories of left and right, as outlined in Chapter 1. However, over the course of *The Third Way and its Critics* (2000) and in the edited *Global Third Way Debate* (2001), as well as in journalistic contributions, Giddens moved away from the functional response towards both the updating values and historical confluence positions. Thus, following Labour's 2001 General Election victory, he suggested that:

> The transition from Labour to new Labour was never a matter of succumbing to the vagaries of the markets. It was a question of creating a party that would *sustain most of the classic concerns of the left, but bring these into line with the demands of a new world.* [emphasis added][30]

Giddens' transition was complete in his *Progressive Manifesto* (2003), in which he moved into the value-led category with an appeal to 'create more *deep support* for left of centre policies ... touching an emotional chord among citizens, not just appealing to their pragmatic interests'.[31] I suggest that the reason for this change lies in the realisation that the functional approach is inadequate for forming a political strategy – a process which necessitates dialogue, flexibility and engagement with conflicting interests and value orientations. Giddens' sociological account of the transformation of left/right concerns the structural function of politics *per se*, rather than the specific, programmatic concerns of the centre-left. Perceiving this, Giddens has since taken time to show how the Third Way project is anchored in social democracy, rather than transcending politics altogether.

However, the second and third positions are similarly insufficient for developing political programmes. The updating values approach seeks to adapt social democracy to meet new challenges, while staying true to an enduring ethos. Yet, this neglects how the content of core political values has always been contested. The approach solidifies values as being immutable in the same way that the functional response does social processes. For example, underlying goals such as 'equality' or 'opportunity' have historically been subject to vastly different interpretations among Labour supporters. Related to this, the notion of updating means to better serve enduring ends neglects the reciprocal relations that ends and means can have in political programmes.[32] In the case of the transition from old to new Labour, the classic example concerns the role of the state. Third Wayers claim that the state need not own key industries or operate public services, on the grounds that 'what matters is what works'. On this view, the enduring social democratic ends have always been the provision of high-quality public services for all; it doesn't matter if the means to achieving such ends involve using the private sector. This neglects the extent to which, for the statist tradition in Labour, state ownership was not just a means of delivery. Common ownership also represented an *end* in the form of the expression of the collective will and interest of society, or even of a particular group (the working class) within that society. The separation of ends and means, implied by the updating values position, thus hides a more complex picture.

The third position, of a historical confluence between social democratic values and social conditions, is the weakest in that it combines the worst aspects of the first two. As with the updating values perspective, the supposedly enduring social democratic values are in a highly particularised form – but are presented as being universal. In terms of social change, the historical confluence position, like the functional response, reifies social conditions at the expense of political agency. In addition, it also seems to adopt an 'end of history' approach that presents current circumstances as being permanent. It is compelled to do this as, having wedded the Third Way to a particular historical conjuncture, a change in that conjuncture would necessarily call into the question the viability of the Third Way response. This is a precarious position indeed for a political strategy.

This leaves the final position, of the primacy of values and political leadership. This approach creates the largest space for political agency, and therefore for forging alternatives. If dominant social trends are the result of political decisions, grounded in values, then contesting such values could lead to alternative strategies and, ultimately, alternative social outcomes. However, in isolation even this agent-centred position is insufficient for reconstructing the Third Way. Chapter 2 criticised purely normative accounts of the Third Way as being ideocentric, and neglecting the importance of material context. The same applies to any approach that emphasises a particular set of values, abstracted from the empirical context in which they will be operationalised. Neglecting this context makes it unlikely that such values will resonate with a wider public. New Labour's ever-shifting lists of its 'core values' look increasingly vacuous with each attempt. Gordon Brown's (2004) 'liberty, duty and fairness'[33] manages to sound even more conservative than Blair's (1998) 'equal worth, opportunity and responsibility'.[34] Efforts to reconstruct the Third Way purely on the basis of supposedly preferable values (e.g. calls for the refoundation of 'real' Labour) are equally misguided. Endless lists of values seem as if plucked from thin air, or like they are being preached at the electorate.

Part I of the book has revealed a tension in Third Way discourse that, as we shall see in Part II, is replicated by many of its critics. On the one hand, Chapter 1 showed that Third Way theory invokes social change as constraining, to the extent that it undermines and reconfigures the categories of left and right. This is embodied in the functional approach identified above, that sees values as being entirely driven by pre-given social conditions. However, Chapter 1 also identified a space in which left and right are actively recombined by political actors. Third Way attempts at such recombination were evident in the normative agenda outlined in Chapter 2, in extreme cases working with *a priori* notions such as 'equal worth'. There is thus a significant dichotomy in Third Way theory. The social processes underpinning the Third Way are treated as given, and yet we know that such processes bear the imprint of political values and choices. Simultaneously, Third Way values are presented as fixed and enduring, but it is clear that they are contested and shaped by their historical and social context.

Sociologically driven accounts emphasise constraints upon the activities of centre-left governments. This neglects where such constraints were politically constructed and, consequently, can be modified. At the other extreme, value-based approaches posit Third Way values in a vacuum from their social context, emptying them of substantive meaning. Any attempt to reconstruct the Third Way which is purely values-based will be subject to the same problem. A viable alternative must engage with the kinds of social processes outlined in Chapter 1, *and* develop a normative account that is grounded in those processes. It is against this benchmark that the Third Way's many critics on the left are outlined and assessed in Part II.

Part II
The Left Critics

4
Neo-Marxists: *Capitalism with an (In)human Face*

What can broadly be labelled neo-Marxist approaches to the Third Way encompass a diverse range of critics. However, they are united by a shared perception of politics as being (to varying degrees) determined by economic and class relations. There is an unlikely similarity between Third Way and neo-Marxist analysis, in that both privilege 'extra-political' factors. Neo-Marxists are concerned with the changing structure of capitalist economic organisation, the recomposition of class relations and how these are reflected at the level of politics. Third Way theorists, while certainly not using the language of Marxism, are similarly concerned with the impact of social and economic change on the scope for political action. This shared theoretical terrain may account for the fact that while neo-Marxists are, in political terms, perhaps the most dismissive of the Third Way, they have nevertheless maintained a sustained critical engagement with it. Neo-Marxist assessments of the Third Way's sociological claims take two main forms. The first rejects the Third Way account of contemporary social change out of hand. The second recognises that major shifts have occurred, but attributes them to the recomposition of an enduring system of capitalist accumulation, for which the Third Way is the latest political vehicle. These two strands of the neo-Marxist critique are discussed below in terms of their assessment of globalisation, the emergence of the knowledge economy and the relationship between social class and political action – all of which are core concerns underpinning the Third Way.

Sociological conditions

Globalisation

Neo-Marxist critics, like Third Wayers themselves, identify globalisation as central to the project of the reformist left. Callinicos notes that, '[Giddens'] accounts of the social world are relentlessly monolithic in their reductionism of social phenomena to the consequences of globalization.'[1] However, neo-Marxist interpretations of globalisation either refute claims as to its quantitative and qualitative novelty altogether, or present it as simply a logical step in the development of capitalism, the core basic features of which remain intact.

The 'rejectionists' challenge the processes identified by Giddens and others on empirical grounds. The extent of economic globalisation is revealed to be greatly exaggerated if measured, for example, in terms of the structure and proportion of world trade.[2] Consequently, the nation-state is presented as still having considerable autonomy in economic policy-making. Indeed, some argue that economic globalisation represents a *strengthening* of national sovereignty. As Bromley argues:

> Not only has the nation-state form expanded with the development of the international economy, but the number as well as the dominance of liberal powers has steadily grown. The expansion of liberal states in the world economy, their participation in international organizations, and the development of international law are not threats to sovereignty, but rather the forms of its consolidation on an increasingly global basis.[3]

In the view of the rejectionists, the discourse of globalisation is a political device used to justify regressive domestic measures, such as the retrenchment of welfare and employment rights.[4] Overall, they argue that 'the Third Way project is flawed in concept partly because it has assimilated the New Times claims about epochal change and applied them to an economy whose problems and contradictions are better understood in other [neo-Marxist] terms'.[5]

A second approach recognises quantitative indicators as to the emergence of a global economy, but denies that this represents the new kind of society pointed to by its more sanguine prophets. Instead, the global economy is located in terms of the long-term development of capitalism. Structuralist versions of this approach locate globalisation as part of a long-term historical trend towards a more interrelated global economy, which an ever-expanding capitalist system has always been moving towards. On this view, globalisation is entirely consistent with the Marxian account of capitalism as 'a revolutionary mode of production whose restless progress subverts traditional institutions and subjects the entire planet to its cycles of creative destruction'.[6] The inherent tendency of capital is to expand, dissolving and reconstituting social relations (in this case, the autonomous nation-state) as it does so.

Alternatively, a more voluntarist account sees nothing inevitable about economic globalisation, and attributes it to the decisions of elite political and business actors on behalf of capital. Benton, also pointing to the domestic political context of globalisation discourse, and in a rebuff to those who see globalisation as having a logic of its own, suggests that:

> So far as governments of the New Right have been concerned, deregulation has been consistent with their economic ideology, and has greatly empowered them in their attempts to weaken labour movements and reduce state sponsorship of social provision *within* their national boundaries ... In short, 'globalisation' is an important strategic weapon in the hands of politically and economically powerful groups and institutional complexes, not a secular tendency of a certain phase of 'modernity'.[7]

On this view, globalisation is a willed project to further particular (ruling class) interests. To be sure, globalisation follows the imperatives of capital accumulation identified in the more structural account. However, it is only because of the ascendancy of certain social groups at a particular time, 'the tipping of the balance of class forces in favour of the owners of capital', that globalisation has been able to proceed apace and in the specific neoliberal form that it has.[8] The question of the balance of class forces is returned to below.

The knowledge economy and class structure

Chapter 1 showed how Third Wayers identify the emergence of a knowledge economy and the collapse of the traditional class structure as redefining the concerns of the left. Neo-Marxists again either challenge such shifts on empirical grounds, or locate them in the context of the recomposition of an enduring system of capitalist social relations.[9]

Rejectionists suggest that the alleged decline of the working class, owing to technological changes, is a chimera. The persistence of the 'old' manufacturing economy is pointed to, alongside continuing, deepening social inequalities along demonstrably class lines.[10] Where changes are acknowledged to have taken place, these are not recognised as representing a new type of economy and society. New communications technologies and production techniques are not given the causal primacy that they are in Third Way accounts. Rather, it is the continual drive towards profit maximisation that spurs technological and organisational innovation. The profit imperative also necessitates the restructuring of the labour market. As Froud *et al.* argue, 'the concept of capitalist accumulation trajectory is more important than any notion of epochal transition'.[11]

Neo-Marxists are particularly scornful of Third Way claims regarding the decline of manual labour and the rise of the so-called 'wired worker'. Giddens suggests that as many as one-third of workers in the EU are wired-workers involved in 'problem-solving activities rather than repetitive tasks'.[12] For neo-Marxists, as long as the wage-labour form still exists, a proletariat that must sell its labour to capitalists can always be identified: 'capital is [still] constituted by its contradictory relationship with wage-labour'.[13] In addition, considerable power differentials exist *between* different types of worker in the knowledge economy. With regard to the content of labour, the apparent rise of 'knowledge jobs' in industrial societies has often simply displaced 'sweatshop' labour to developing economies.[14] Furthermore, much of the work that goes on in the knowledge economy is de-skilled, routinised and chronically insecure.[15] Indeed, such insecurity can be seen as a form of the continuing domination of capital over labour.[16] These various criticisms are summarised by McLennan's challenge to Giddens' 'contestable sociology':

> Why should we take it as inevitable that most people in most nations will become wired workers of the requisite type? And why should we assume – where is the qualitative research to *show*? – that current wired workers are really satisfied problem-solvers rather than agitated repetitive taskers? And how many really work

in non-hierarchical environments, whatever that means? On the contrary, there is much to suggest that truly 'wired workers' in Giddens's sense are a small minority, and that the larger majority of wired and unwired workers alike are increasingly stressed, audited, monitored, prone to all manner of new health risks and, yes, severely underpaid too, given their rather modest attempts to construct enviable 'lifestyles'.[17]

From the neo-Marxist perspective there is still an industrial working class (or equivalent) that, as the dominated group in an exploitative system, has the capacity to be mobilised against it. Thus, despite recognising the significance of new oppositional movements such as the anti-globalisers, Callinicos concludes that the revolutionary social transformation to a more humane society requires:

> the development of a mass movement *centred on the organized working class* that seeks the democratic reconstruction of society. Only in this way can the centres of concentrated capitalist power in the economy and the state be effectively challenged. [emphasis added][18]

Politics and class

Underpinning the neo-Marxist critique of Third Way sociology is an account of a shift in the balance of class forces. This highlights the intensification of capitalist accumulation through economic globalisation, the deregulation of the labour market and the retrenchment of post-war progressive measures in social policy. These developments are held to reflect both the strengthening of the traditional capitalist class, as well as the emergence of a new fraction of that class at the level of politics: embodied in the modernisation of social democratic parties in particular.

In analyses of what might be labelled the traditional capitalist class, economic globalisation on neoliberal terms represents the re-emergence and consolidation of this group's social power.[19] The post-war period saw the ascendance of the working class, with electoral victories and the establishment of social democratic welfare regimes. Crouch has located this shift in historical perspective, suggesting that 'In a very real sense the post-war decades were the decades of the working classes of the industrial world.'[20] However, the numerical decline of the working class, the emergence of new technologies, increasingly efficient management practices, the rise of neoliberal political parties and the centrality of shareholder value above other criteria put the capitalist class back into the ascendancy.[21]

Another class-centred feature of the neo-Marxist analysis is an explanation of recent developments in centre-left parties, including the appearance of the Third Way, in terms of the emergence of a particular class fraction. The modernisation of New Labour represents the ascendance of what Gilbert refers to as the 'technical–financial–management elite' within the Labour movement and those who influence it.[22] What might be called the 'embourgeoisement' of Labour Party machinery is suggested by Webb and Fisher's study of the socioeconomic profile of Labour's HQ staff which concludes that 'Employees in the contemporary Labour Party are mainly white, middle class, well educated and young to middle-aged.' The study also notes how the orientation of employees reflects a new 'political entrepreneurialism'.[23] Crouch's work suggests such entrepreneurialism is embodied in individuals who 'even though sympathetic to the party and its goals, work for it primarily for money', as well as 'pure professionals, who are hired by the party to do a job, and who may not necessarily be its political supporters'.[24] Crucially, all such individuals tend to have close links to business interests seeking a political presence.

Two implications flow from this account of a particular class fraction coming to dominate Labour politics. The first is that the Third Way discourse of the inevitability of globalisation, the knowledge economy and the other 'realities' of contemporary politics that it describes are in fact the direct expression of a particular class interest. Bourdieu and Wacquant describe such imaginaries as 'the social fantasies of the dominant' which are 'endowed with the performative power to bring into being the very realities it claims to describe, according to the principle of the self-fulfilling prophecy'.[25] As Gilbert suggests:

> This is the politics of the Third Way: an insistence that there is no alternative to a global economic settlement in which the technocrats of the managerial class wield all power. What is crucial to recognise is the fact that the people telling us this have a vested interest in it being so. They are not merely reporting a situation, but creating one.[26]

The second implication is an apparent coincidence of interests between the class fraction that has come to dominate centre-left politics, and the key electoral demographic that centre-left parties must appeal to. On this account, the upwardly mobile yet culturally conservative worldview of the New Labour elite is compatible with the outlook of the 'Middle England' demographic it targets. The Third Way thus represents 'the politics of the classes who have done well out of the dissolution of the post-war settlement'.[27] Additionally, Froud *et al.* suggest that Third Way economic strategies, forged in the context of a sustained consumer boom, rely on continued middle-class spending power for their success. They conclude that:

> it is perhaps entirely fitting that a Labour leadership which has separated the party from what remains of the organised working class should now depend economically as well as politically on the middle classes whose lifestyles and aspirations it shares.[28]

Neo-Marxists also use a class analysis to suggest how the Third Way might be resisted. Two strategies are apparent, again reflecting a tendency to either reject the Third Way's sociological claims, or to acknowledge them as part of a capitalist restructuring. In the rejectionist tendency, centre-left parties are criticised for abandoning the working class at precisely the moment they could be mobilised against widening inequalities and the social effects of neoliberalism. Commenting during the early stages of the transition to New Labour, Benton observed that 'there is a paradox. As the case against capital becomes ever more powerful and urgent, socialism is at its lowest ebb for a century or more.'[29] Similarly, Marxist historian Eric Hobsbawm points to the irony of New Labour enthusiastically embracing neoliberalism, just when the limits of that project were becoming manifest. He asks if New Labour is 'prepared to recognise that the economic theory, or the excuses, it inherited from its [Conservative] predecessor, are going down the tubes?'[30] Alternatively, those who acknowledge that traditional class politics has declined, seek new agents to challenge the capitalist order. They reason that in the process of capitalist restructuring, the sites of resistance will have also been reconstituted. Given that the key capitalist restructuring process has been globalisation, a favourite candidate to redefine revolutionary social agency is thus the anti-globalisation movement. Callinicos holds out the hope that 'those engaged in different kinds of collective action are increasingly motivated by a sense that, beyond their specific concerns or grievances, lies a common enemy – global capitalism'.[31]

Summary: neo-Marxists and the character of the Third Way

Both the Third Way and its neo-Marxist critics seek to explore political possibilities in the context of an assessment of social and economic conditions. Neo-Marxists tend either to challenge the empirical validity of Third Way claims, or accept that significant change has occurred but locate it in the context of capitalist restructuring. In addition, they attempt to demonstrate the enduring reflection of capitalist class relations at the level of politics. Given this, neo-Marxist responses to the Third Way can be seen as the latest instalment in a long-standing radical critique of a reformist politics attempting to manage the 'symptoms' of capitalism, rather than challenge its basic structure.

Where neo-Marxists reject Third Way sociology, the project itself is portrayed as having little or no substance in its own right. The Third Way is seen simply as an elaborate rhetorical device for legitimising the capitulation of the centre-left to neoliberalism, 'an ideological façade behind which capitalism continues on its brutal and destructive way'.[32] It achieves this by, in effect, appropriating for neoliberalism the vocabulary of social democracy, and bandaging the wounds of the market's most damaging effects with limited welfare and regeneration policies. The Third Way is thus viewed as merely an exercise in semantic engineering.[33] From this perspective, Giddens and other Third Wayers have simply reconciled themselves with neoliberalism, looking to 'adapt to the existing order, seeking marginal improvements inflated by self-deceiving rhetoric'.[34]

The above position represents a 'die-hard' tendency in neo-Marxist analysis, that seeks to demonstrate the persistence of the contours of industrial capitalism. However, we have seen that there is also a variant on this approach, giving greater credence to Third Way sociology. Rather than seeing the Third Way as a smokescreen or relatively passive conduit for capitalist interests, it ascribes to the project a more aggressive role. The Third Way not only legitimises the neoliberal hegemony, but is a strategy for its active reinforcement, promotion and development. In this vein, Cammack suggests that the Third Way represents a:

> 'second-phase' neo-liberal approach which moves on from initial short-term 'shock-treatment', aimed at dismantling structures hostile to the operation of markets, to the construction for the longer term of enduring institutions which will sustain markets and capitalist disciplines into the future.[35]

Furthermore, dressed up as it is in the language of the centre-left, the Third Way is able to extend the dominance of capital, through deregulation and privatisation, in ways that would hitherto have been off-limits to traditional Conservatives and even neoliberals. As Callinicos concludes, 'Far from breaking with the neoliberal policies of the New Right, [the Third Way] has continued and, in certain ways, radicalized them.'[36]

Implications for left/right

Chapter 1 suggested that Third Way sociology points to the categories of left and right being undermined altogether, reconfigured in line with structural changes, or actively recombined by agents pursuing new political projects. There is a similarity between Third Way and neo-Marxist analysis, in tending to see politics as determined by economic and social conditions. Related to this, there are further, doubtless unintended, similarities between neo-Marxist and Third Way accounts of the status of left and right.

In the rejectionist neo-Marxist response, which refutes the empirical claims of the Third Way, left and right are *undermined* to the extent that they are something of an irrelevance in the face of wider, enduring capitalist structures. The Third Way is seen as a semantic smokescreen, without substance in its own right. It illustrates the irrelevance of the categories of left and right within a capitalist framework, by signifying their final collapse into one another, 'capitalism ... becomes a second nature, the inescapable horizon of social life in the modern world'.[37] Alternative neo-Marxist responses, which take seriously both the Third Way and new social conditions, tend to see a *reconfiguration* or an *active recombination* of left and right. Having identified the Third Way as a capitalist offensive, such analyses imply that it is a vehicle through which the neoliberal right have colonised the social democratic left. The purpose of this is to expand market logic into all areas of society, 'what can best be designated perhaps as neoliberalism's "passive revolutionary phase"'.[38] This indicates a *reconfiguration* of left and right, as it is not that these categories have become redundant, but rather that the right has at least temporarily 'won out' through dragging the left–right axis rightwards. This shift is described by Lester, who suggests that the Third Way has:

> Situated itself between the 'extremes' of an earlier, already perceived, right-wing version of social democracy and a right-wing form of conservatism ... As a consequence, whatever aspirations it claims to have in terms of 'renewing' social democracy, by its very nature it has shifted the 'centre ground' of politics way to the right of where it previously stood.[39]

The *recombination* of left and right is observed by neo-Marxists in the same sense that it is by Third Wayers, but obviously assessed in a negative light. Thus, like Giddens, neo-Marxists see Third Wayers turning to the 'radicalism' of the market as part of the recombination of left/ right themes. However, neo-Marxists analyse this move in terms of an extension of neoliberal capitalist interests, rather than as the vehicle for progressive modernisation. Similarly, where Giddens points critically to the 'conservatism of radicals' through their defence of outmoded institutions such as the post-war welfare state, neo-Marxists are aware that they have found some unlikely allies (liberals, one-nation Tories) in the political space reconfigured by the Third Way.[40] Thus, criticising the privileging of responsibilities over rights, as a reversal of even basic liberal tenets, Callinicos notes that:

> I invoke the classical liberal argument in favour of rights with some embarrassment. Things have come to a pretty pass when a Marxist has to remind defenders of contemporary Western liberal societies of the point of concepts constitutive of liberalism itself.[41]

This observation encapsulates the effect that the recombination of left and right, in a newly reconfigured political space, has upon neo-Marxist critics as much as Third Wayers themselves. Liberalism, the traditional opponent of Marxism, suddenly looks appealing to Marxists as a defence of core progressive values.

Assessment: sociological-value relations

What does the neo-Marxist analysis of the role of Third Way politics, in the context of social and economic change, imply about the relations between social conditions and political values? Chapter 3 noted that of the four types of claim regarding such relations in the Third Way, no single account ever tends to dominate. Instead, simultaneous and often contradictory claims are implied. Neo-Marxist critiques similarly suggest a mixture of the different types of relationship between material conditions and political action.

In neo-Marxist responses it is what was identified in Chapter 3 as the *functional* relationship between social change and political values that looms large. Political interventions appear as predetermined by prior structures: in this case the impersonal logic of capital accumulation. This view is illustrated by Watkins' detailed analysis in the *New Left Review* of New Labour's record in government, which concludes that 'It is an anachronism to think that the performance of rival parties *competing within the field of neoliberal politics* can be distinguished, once in office, by their ideological pedigrees or electoral bases' [emphasis added].[42] Despite this spectre, the other types of relations identified in Chapter 3 are also present. The *historical confluence* position, which implies a fit between enduring centre-left values and the present historical conjuncture, appears to a limited extent. Neo-Marxists hold that reformist centre-left strategies, and indeed democratic politics in general, have *always* been about managing the tensions and restructuring of capitalism: the confluence between the Third Way and neoliberal globalisation simply serves to illustrate this.[43] More significant is the presence of the position which sees the Third Way as centre-left ideas being *updated* to meet the demands of new times. Neo-Marxists certainly agree with this, but not in the positive sense meant by Third Wayers. For neo-Marxists, the 'updating' of social democratic values into the Third Way is merely the development of an appropriate discourse to manage the recomposition of capitalism. This, again, is an explanation that leans towards the functionalist position in its deferral to the permanence of capitalist structures prior to political interventions.

More complicated is the relationship between neo-Marxist critiques and the final position identified in Chapter 3, which gives *primacy to agency* and the role of norms and values in politics. Thus far it has been shown how neo-Marxists ultimately veer towards the functionalist, structurally dependent position. However, there is ambiguity concerning the question of agency in the class-based explanation of Third Way politics. This reflects an older debate concerning the relationship between capital, class and the state in Marxist theory. The ambiguity applies to both the account of elites in constructing the Third Way, and the agency of those who might resist it. We have seen that neo-Marxist perspectives that acknowledge the 'new times' see them as part of a capitalist offensive, and one dimension of the neo-Marxist critique is its identification of the Third Way with the interests of a particular fraction of the dominant class. The very expression 'capitalist offensive' suggests a deliberate, active strategy on the part of a particular group of agents. However, there is a lack of clarity concerning whether these agents are effectively 'dupes', unable to act other than according to the logic of their role within the structure of capitalism, or whether they are granted more agency than this. In the latter scenario, actors have *chosen* to pursue Third Way strategies based on conviction, an assessment of self-interest or some similar criteria. Consequently, the cry against the leadership of centre-left parties and their intellectual allies is often one of *betrayal* of the socialist cause.[44] However, betrayal implies that those agents could have acted differently, thus ascribing choice and agency to the ruling group. This then calls into question the efficacy of the functional (and other) explanations offered by the neo-Marxists, that privilege structural dependency upon capital. If it is simply the *decisions* of political elites that are wrong, it is not capitalism as such that determines the content of political strategies, but the orientation of the governing classes. A change of heart by ruling elites, rather than the transformation of the capitalist system, would be sufficient for a meaningful change of political direction.

In the case of resistance to the Third Way, neo-Marxists retain faith in the agency of a revolutionary class, whether in the form of a traditional proletariat, or new agents such as the anti-globalisation movement. However, they underplay how the kinds of social processes pointed to in Third Way sociology have diminished, or at least radically altered, the capacity of the working class to be mobilised. As Watkins acknowledges, 'After twenty years of neoliberalism, the British working class itself has been transformed ... Its capacities for collective action have visibly waned.'[45] In addition, those who do recognise the extent of this change, and put their faith in new agents such as the anti-globalisers, neglect that the objectives of such groups may be radically different to those of the traditional working class – and may even go against them. This is evident, for example, in the potential for tension between globally focused environmentalists, and nationally oriented labour activists seeking to protect jobs in polluting, heavy industries.

Conclusion

Like the Third Way, its neo-Marxist critics seek to understand politics in the context of economic and social change. Viewing the contemporary social terrain, neo-Marxists make their own assessment of (alleged) processes such as globalisation and the rise of a knowledge economy. Their account, unsurprisingly given the heritage of their critique, focuses heavily on the dynamics of class relations. Two broad neo-Marxist responses to Third Way sociology were identified: rejectionist accounts which challenge the empirical veracity of Third Way claims, and those which acknowledge radical changes but locate them as part of the recomposition of an enduring capitalist system. The former tend to see the Third Way as merely a smokescreen for an enduring neoliberal capitalism, while the latter observe a more active role for the Third Way in extending and entrenching it.

Neo-Marxist critiques have been shown to reproduce a number of the analytical assumptions that were attributed to the Third Way itself. Consequently, they are by themselves insufficient for developing alternatives. Where such critiques do not buy into Third Way claims as to the redundancy of left and right, they adopt ideas about these categories that reflect the static understanding of the left–right axis that was criticised in Chapter 2. Thus, for example, 'left' remains constituted by ideas about proletarian agency and the transition to socialism. In addition, neo-Marxist understandings of the relationship between social change and political agency reproduce each of the categories that were identified as inadequate in this respect in Chapter 3. Even where the novelty of social change is recognised (the 'new times'), it is still assessed against a model developed very much under 'old times'. These criticisms of neo-Marxist approaches are discussed further in Chapter 7, in relation to the other critical perspectives on the Third Way that will be assessed. At the same time, the *strengths* of neo-Marxist approaches will be identified as their ability to link the Third Way to material interests and power relations, and to maintain the importance of a left/right distinction through a critique of the market.

5
Anti-Technocrats: *The Tyranny of Targets*

Chapter 1 showed how a key tenet of Third Way social theory is that social change has led to the redundancy, or at least the marginalisation, of the categories of left and right. It is this new 'post-ideological' climate that is held to be the starting point for evidence-based Third Way policy-making. This is encapsulated in the New Labour mantra of 'what matters is what works', revealing a stated preference for practical rather than ideological solutions in government. A group of responses to the Third Way shares this analysis of its technocratic element, but from an entirely critical perspective – here I label them 'anti-technocrats'. The anti-technocratic position is reminiscent of the Frankfurt School critique of politics in industrial societies, although the disparate critics discussed in this chapter do not explicitly align themselves with that tradition.[1] They include political scientists focusing on depoliticisation as a governing strategy, as well as theorists of governmentality and the construction of new types of political subject. The radical democratic critique of the Third Way, which criticises its attempt to eradicate antagonism, might also be included under this heading but is pursued in more detail in Chapter 7.

The key distinction between anti-technocratic and neo-Marxist approaches is that whereas the latter focus on capital accumulation and class struggle, anti-technocrats problematise rationality itself. The space for debate about social and political alternatives is held to be increasingly eroded by an instrumental, technocratic reason. The only goal of such reason is the reduction of all areas of social life, politics included, to the administration of what are narrowly regarded as the most efficient techniques.[2] Neo-Marxist critics were shown to lack clarity with regard to the amount of agency possessed by both promoters of the Third Way and potential resisting groups, in the context of an enduring system of capitalist relations. The anti-technocratic perspective is better able to address the *political* processes, beyond just the economic, that underpin the Third Way. This is due to a focus on the mechanisms of governing that embody the rationalisation and technicisation of politics. However, over the question of the relationship between this technocratic logic, and the space for developing political alternatives to the Third Way, anti-technocrats encounter similar limitations to the neo-Marxists.

Sociological conditions

As with the neo-Marxists, anti-technocrats identify the importance of similar social changes to Third Wayers. However, these processes are not analysed primarily in terms of capitalist restructuring and accumulation strategies, as they are in neo-Marxist political economy, although such aspects are not neglected. Instead, anti-technocrats have a more 'political' concern, in the sense that they concentrate on what we might call the mode of government. Thus, the key areas identified below as preoccupying the anti-technocrats involve the development of the bureaucratic, technocratic welfare state; changes in the relationship between political parties, the electorate and the state; and the reconfiguration of governing techniques at the level of culture.

Development of the technocratic welfare state

It was shown in Chapters 1 and 2 how welfare reform is central to the Third Way. In particular, this involves transforming the state's role from that of a direct provider to an enabler, both of people (for example, through welfare to work) and of services (for example, facilitating public–private partnerships). Neo-Marxists locate shifts of this sort in the context of capitalist restructuring. For anti-technocrats, however, Third Way welfare reforms are theorised in the context of the long-term development of an increasingly widespread technocratic rationality. This is characterised in two potentially contradictory senses, which imply different understandings of the extent of technocratic rationality and the possibility of resisting it. On the one hand, technocratic Third Way interventions are presented as part of a long-term trend in modernity – the continual development and refining of managerial techniques and strategies. What Marcuse saw as the reduction of politics to 'technics' is characterised in large part by a seemingly obsessive urge to measure and quantify.[3] Rose describes this tendency as 'a dream of the technocratic control of the accidental by continuous monitoring and management of risk'.[4] There is no doubt that the setting of targets and measuring of performance at even the most micro-level has been a feature of Third Way governing strategies, and is well documented in the case of New Labour in particular.[5] As Terranova surmises:

> This quest for precision, the conviction that knowledge of all the variables will inevitably lead to better performance, is a particularly strong obsession of bureaucracies and one which has not disappeared but become exaggerated in a phenomenon such as Blairism.[6]

A second view presents Third Way managerialism as merely the latest inadequate response to previous bureaucratic, interventionist failure. Commenting on the US situation in particular, Frankel observes that:

> the unintended consequences of social pathologies necessitate ever growing bureaucratic intervention. However, this intervention is counter-productive in that it strengthens the very conditions that gave rise to administrative intervention – poor productivity, motivation, rationality and so forth.[7]

On this account, in the flexible, information economy identified by the Third Way, in which hierarchical, command and control systems are redundant, obsessive measurement is in fact *inefficient*. As Terranova notes:

> measurement of all the variables is not in itself enough to increase the performativity of the system. It just does not work that way; the more knowledge is generated about a system the more the uncertainty.[8]

The result is a spiral of inefficiency in large-scale bureaucracies. Under pressure to 'do something' about the public services, policy-makers devise increasingly interventionist strategies of target-setting, data collection and measurement which are entirely inappropriate to those services. Consequently, the seeming inefficiency of public services, in comparison to their market-oriented private sector counterparts, is intensified.

On the one hand, then, anti-technocrats locate Third Way strategies for transforming the role of the state in the context of a long-term tendency – towards politics becoming increasingly technocratic. This account leans towards the rather bleak prognosis originally offered by Marcuse for the 'totally administered society', which obliterates the possibility of politics as a meaningful dialogue about social futures.[9] Alternatively, the presentation of Third Way interventions as a reactive, crisis-management response to the cumulative *failures* of the bureaucratic state, which are themselves doomed to fail by deploying inappropriate monitoring strategies, implies that the totally administered society can never be realised. The repeated failure of intervention strategies opens up spaces for opposition. This is illustrated by antagonism over New Labour's attempts to 'micro-manage' public services, a tendency which opponents on left and right see as a political vulnerability.

Changing relations between electorate, parties and state

Chapter 1 showed that a core Third Way assumption is of class and partisan dealignment amongst the electorate. Anti-technocrats have identified this as having a de-ideologising effect upon party programmes; part of a wider shift in the nature of political parties in late-capitalist countries. In order to achieve electoral success, parties have to move from being based on a sectional interest (for example, the working class) to appealing to as broad a section of the electorate as possible. Achieving this involves the inclusion of multiple coalition partners in any party project.

The electoral strategy which follows from these preconditions was captured in the 1960s by Otto Kircheimer's ideal-type of the 'catch-all' party.[10] The elements of this ideal-type are evident in the development of New Labour. Firstly, Kircheimer identified the explicit dropping of ideological baggage. This was symbolised by New Labour's infamous rewriting of Clause IV of its constitution, which had committed it to common ownership of the means of production.

Secondly, the 'catch-all' party leader is strengthened and projected as a *national* leader, who transcends sectional interests. This is exemplified in Blair's constant invocation of 'the people' as his constituency, whom he appeals to directly, above sectional interests.[11] Blair is widely seen as having the strongest grip by any Labour leader over his party, rooted in the party reforms initiated by Kinnock in the 1980s. This, combined with Blair's style of decision-making in government, has led to his leadership being frequently characterised as 'presidential'. The strengthening of the party leadership has been paralleled by a dramatic downgrading of the importance of party members in policy formation, despite leadership claims to be further involving them.[12]

The third element of Kircheimer's 'catch-all' party is the attempt to appeal to as wide a section of the electorate as possible. New Labour strategists developed a focus on specific, market-tested policies and rhetoric tailored to the perceived individual, psychological needs of target voters. This represented a shift away from an analysis of voters' 'objective' ideological interests, such as those that are held to be determined by class location.[13] This strategy is embodied in New Labour's targeting of 'Middle England', and is particularly evident in all-inclusive rhetorical formations such as the pledge to govern 'for all our people'. Finally, Kircheimer identified the need for the catch-all party to broaden the range of interest groups to which it has access. This was illustrated by New Labour's famous 'prawn-cocktail offensive', of courting leading City figures, prior to the 1997 general election.

Writing in the 1960s, Kircheimer identified the shift to being a catch-all party as the *only* means for the former mass parties to achieve electoral success in a 'de-ideologised' age. This implies that Third Way parties going down the 'catch-all' route are merely *reacting* to the imperatives of social transformations which are beyond their control. However, a far more active portrayal of party 'modernisation' is offered in accounts of Third Way strategy from within contemporary political science. Mair suggests that New Labour have not just passively responded to an external, changing electorate, but that they have actively fostered what he calls a 'partyless democracy'. This is described as a:

coherent, and quite deliberate strategy aimed at transforming democratic governance. At its core, this new strategy is designed not to promote party government but rather to eliminate it: instead of seeking to enhance partisan control, New Labour strategy seems directed towards the creation of a partyless and hence de-politicized democracy.[14]

The components of the 'catch-all' party are actively deployed to bypass the traditional intermediary mechanisms of representative democracy, such as parliament and parties. Instead, the government rules on the basis of claims to have a direct mandate from 'the people'. This is achieved rhetorically through a discourse that purports to speak for the whole community. Practically, the approach is realised through media and marketing techniques which communicate directly with the electorate. Crucially, the architects of this approach, publicly at least, insist that it represents a more responsive and therefore democratic form of government. Labour's senior pollster and focus group manager, Philip Gould, refers to what critics disparagingly call 'government by focus group' as 'continuous democracy'.[15] This is again to the detriment of traditional forms of political organisation, which presumed partisanship and ideological division. As Mair summarises:

> For New Labour, party appears to serve no other purpose than to be the voice of the people writ large. It no longer enjoys its own autonomous agenda. Partisanship in this sense is a thing of the past – both electorally and ideologically ... The relationship of this sense of democracy to the ideology of the Third Way is clear. Just as New Labour sees its programme as the only alternative, and hence without partisan purpose, so too the style of government is deliberately advertised as non-partisan. This is not intended as party democracy. It is government for, and indeed of, the people, rather than of any particular section of that people.[16]

A different perspective on depoliticisation is offered by Burnham who, rather than seeing it as the logical corollary of Third Way ideology, accounts for it as a particular form of statecraft. He defines depoliticisation as:

> the process of placing at one remove the political character of decision-making. State managers retain arm's length control over

crucial economic and social processes whilst simultaneously benefiting from the distancing effects of depoliticisation.[17]

From this perspective, the activities of governments should not be understood in 'simple ideological terms'.[18] Rather, the analytical focus should be on the enduring problems of governance, and the strategies (or forms of statecraft) that are variously employed to tackle them. The ultimate expression of this approach (albeit from a very different perspective) is to be found in the work of governmentality theorists, whose relevance to analysing New Labour's Third Way is detailed below.

Governance through culture

Theories of governmentality represent the most sustained attempt to analyse the technicisation of the functions of the state and its relationship to the citizenry. Drawing explicitly on the substantive and methodological approach of Michel Foucault, governmentality theorists have sought to understand how power circulates at *all* levels of society. Rejecting the traditional separation of state, civil society and economy, political power is understood here not as power *over* but, rather, power *through*. Power is identified and analysed precisely in the development of the concrete, everyday practices and strategies of both those who are ostensibly 'governors' and 'governed'. As Rose and Miller suggest, in their seminal article on the approach:

> Power is not so much a matter of imposing constraints upon citizens as of 'making up' citizens capable of bearing a kind of regulated freedom. Personal autonomy is not the antithesis of political power, but a key term in its exercise, the more so because *most individuals are not merely the subjects of power but play a part in its operations.* [emphasis added][19]

> government is intrinsically linked to the activities of expertise, whose role is not one of weaving an all-pervasive web of 'social control', but of enacting assorted attempts at the calculated administration of diverse aspects of conduct ...[20]

In the governmentality literature, the authors tend not to analyse political programmes in terms of left and right, but rather as generalised problems of government evidenced in the 'rationalities', 'mentalities' and 'technologies' of rule. The focus on how power is constituted through specific governing techniques, and its relationship to expertise, leads to an analysis of programmes enacted by state agencies, businesses and other organisations that seek to act upon the social body in some form. Rose maps out specifically how work in the governmentality tradition can be used to understand the Third Way project.[21] He locates the Third Way as representative of a wider shift towards an 'ethopolitics', in which the new object of governance is the actual 'ethical formation and self-management of individuals'.[22] On this terrain, the extent and depth of the exercise of power is taken to new levels:

> ethopower, works through the values, beliefs and sentiments thought to underpin the techniques of responsible self-government and the management of one's obligations to others. In ethopolitics, life itself, in its everyday manifestations, is the object of adjudication.[23]

This account of a new mode of governance clearly resonates with core Third Way themes, in particular that of the enabling state, and its mission to empower communities. The 'community' invoked as part of this discourse is not some given entity which government can act upon. Instead, government actively *constructs* community as a site upon which citizens can be controlled: *'government through community'*.[24] By ostensibly empowering citizens to help themselves, the Third Way strategy is in fact one of displacing problems of government from the level of the state to that of the individual: governance becomes fully internalised.[25] As Rose summarises:

> governing through communities involves establishing relations between the moral values of communities and those of individual citizens. Of course, practices of citizen formation are not themselves new, but what is perhaps novel is the attention paid to citizens as autonomous individuals who must actively construct a life through the practical choices they make about their conduct, and who must bear individual responsibility for the nature and consequences of those choices.[26]

A number of critiques of the Third Way confirm the insight of governmentality theorists that contemporary governing strategies seek to construct a new type of political subject. Finlayson suggests that 'Underlying [New Labour's] proposals is a clear moralisation, but one that can be understood as feeding into a strategy of governance aiming to change the culture and outlook of those it touches.'[27] Often, critics identify the subject under construction as one appropriate to an era of flexible production and capital accumulation, revealing some affinity with neo-Marxist perspectives. Thus, Finlayson argues that 'Culture ... becomes the terrain upon which citizen-subjects will be managed and produced, inducing a form of citizenship that is essentially in harmony with the economy.'[28] This view is elaborated by Rustin, who identifies New Labour's debt to Foucault's notion of 'the governance of souls' and suggests:

> 'Individualisation' has become, in effect, a positive goal of public policy. *It is deemed to be a functional requirement of a successful capitalist economy* that citizens acquire the competencies and mentalities to compete in the modern labour market ... The doctrine of 'no rights without responsibilities' ... signifies that individuals whether they like it or not must be constructed as self-reliant and responsible citizens ... [emphasis added][29]

It is ironic that while the Third Way seeks to construct a subject fit for the demands of new economic imperatives, the very emphasis upon *individual* responsibilities simultaneously obliterates discussion of the role of economic factors in creating social exclusion, community breakdown and other 'problems' identified by the Third Way in the first instance. As Rose notes, 'The unequal distribution of material resources, which had been a target of Left politics since the end of the nineteenth century, gradually blurs as an object of investigation and political action.'[30]

Summary

Like the Third Way and its neo-Marxist critics, anti-technocrats understand politics in the context of macro social developments. However, anti-technocrats place a greater emphasis upon the political elements of the Third Way, as a governing strategy, than neo-Marxists. The focus on the development of the technocratic welfare state, the depoliticising strategies of Third Way parties, and technologies of governance, differs from the neo-Marxist concern with the primacy of economic developments and class relations. However, it is shown below that despite these differences, there are a number of analytical similarities between the two approaches; again, these are in terms of what they imply for our understanding of the categories of left and right, and the relations between social change and political agency. Most significantly, the imperative of technocratic reason can be seen to mirror that of capital accumulation in neo-Marxist accounts.

Implications for left/right

It is the undermining of left and right, rather than their reconfiguring or recombining, which predominates in anti-technocratic accounts. Very much in the tradition of Marcuse's famous depiction of the one-dimensional society, and its 'closing of the political universe', governing is portrayed as having become a mere technical issue, and not a site of political contestation.[31] As Mair suggests:

> There is an increasing tendency to believe that objective solutions to social, economic or cultural problems are most likely to be found after you have established a judicious mix of institutional correctness and expert, non-partisan judgements. Partisanship becomes redundant, democracy de-politicized. This is the ultimate logic of the Third Way approach to governing.[32]

Similarly, in accounts which focus on governmentality and new technologies of rule, ideas about left and right are secondary to the overall mode of governance. The problem is not to assess whether the Third Way is, for example, neoliberal or social democratic, but to understand how it embodies a shift to the individualisation of the process of governing political subjects.

Anti-technocrats diverge from the economic reductionism of neo-Marxists by focusing on the *political* mechanisms of the Third Way as a governing strategy. Paradoxically, though, they are primarily concerned with the *depoliticising* effects of such a strategy; they point to how the Third Way obliterates the categories of left and right through which we have conventionally understood political pro-grammes. The key distinction that emerges among anti-technocrats is between those who see the undermining of left and right, and depoliti-cisation in general, as an (almost) inevitable function of rationality as modernity develops, and those who see it as a willed political strategy. In the case of the latter, the *reconfiguring and recombining* of left and right also come to be involved.

It was shown above that one explanation of the rise of Third Way, technocratic managerialism, was that it is simply the latest in a series of crisis-management interventions by a failing bureaucratic state. The proponents of this approach point to the rise of a 'New Class' to show how such interventions lead to a *reconfiguring* of the left–right axis along different lines. On this account, the traditional capital–labour class struggle is replaced by a political confrontation between 'centralisers' and 'populists'. The centralisers consist of the New Class of welfare professionals, academics and new social movement actors committed to extending the state apparatus to solve social crises. Populists, on the other hand, favour a reduced state, local autonomy and a more participatory democracy.[33] From this perspective, Third Way parties at their most interventionist – especially with their heavy concentration of former public sector professionals – can be seen as the political triumph of the New Class.

What is noteworthy, however, is that this reconfiguration is seen as the result of a history of bureaucratic interventions, unintended consequences, and further interventions apparently beyond the control of the actors involved. For an account that implies a more active *recombination* of the categories of left and right, we need to turn to those who see depoliticisation being deployed as a *deliberate* political strategy. Thus, both Burnham and Mair present depoliticisation as a contemporary method of tackling enduring problems of governance. For Burnham, it is a device to avoid blame for failed economic policies by adopting a 'rules-based' approach. In the case of Mair, depoliticisation is a way of bypassing political debate, especially at the level of the party, and of allowing 'the people' to endorse apparently non-partisan policies. Both strategies might be termed a recombination of left and right into a *populism of the centre*.

Accounts that identify the construction of a particular type of political subject also suggest the recombination of left and right by pointing to how, for example, the traditionally leftist theme of developing human potential can be complementary to the knowledge economy (see Chapter 8). Similarly, community and individual are not seen as opposed; community is the site within which the modern individual is constructed – and ultimately constructs themselves.

This account mirrors the Third Way's own view of the reciprocal relationship between individual and community, but from a critical perspective.

Assessment: sociological-value relations

Of the four types of sociological-normative relations identified in Chapter 3, it is the *functional* account, viewing political values as merely reflecting impersonal social structures, which dominates in anti-technocratic approaches. Anti-technocrats give the sense that Third Way governing strategies represent a wider, long-term trend towards the technicisation of society and politics. Such a trend is apparently inherent in the logic of the development of modern institutions. In its own way, this portrayal of an omnipresent technocratic reason is as deterministic as the most reductionist accounts of both neo-Marxists and Third Way advocates. Crucially, *even the governors themselves* are subject to these wider system imperatives. The primary concern is not that there is a specific preference among Third Way strategists for depoliticising strategies, and for increased use of mechanisms such as public audit. Rather, the logic of their operating environment means they only have to act rationally to reproduce such trends.

The *historical confluence* position is discernible in anti-technocratic accounts which marry the analysis of a colonising, technocratic reason to the contingent factors which have shaped the Third Way. For example, New Labour's tendency towards micro-management and authoritarianism, which is a feature of the idea of a burgeoning technocratic reason, is also often held to be a feature of the statist, labourist tradition which Third Wayers inherited and have held onto.[34] Similarly, the complex structural depoliticising pressures, which are held to have shut down the media as a space for debate about political alternatives, have been intensified in the specific media context of Third Way politics. New Labour had to confront a media that was overwhelmingly hostile to the Labour Party, and thus adopted a strategy of 'total campaigning' in the 1990s. In short, this involved fighting the general election every day of the political cycle. The tactics this entailed have led to repeated charges of 'style over substance', media manipulation and 'spin' – all of which illustrate the anti-technocrats' broader fears of the 'closure of the political universe'. There is thus an historical confluence between the long-term process of societal rationalisation and the more immediate, specific context of the Third Way.

Anti-technocrat versions of the *updating values* approach also mirror those of the neo-Marxists in understanding the Third Way. Anti-technocrats agree with Third Wayers that values are being updated to reflect new times, but evaluate this shift negatively. Thus, we have seen how from this critical perspective 'community' is understood as a value invoked not because of a desire for social solidarity, but as the new terrain upon which governance occurs and political subjects are constructed. Similarly, the discourse of rights and responsibilities is seen not as an attempt to synthesise competing political traditions, but to displace the activity of governance onto individuals themselves. Finally, the *value-led* approach is, ironically, strongly evident in accounts which focus on *depoliticisation* as a deliberate governing strategy. It was noted above that Mair and Burnham, operating from the disciplinary perspective of political science, portray the Third Way as an intentional strategy of depoliticisation, designed, paradoxically, to ultimately *strengthen* government.

Conclusion

Anti-technocrats have a more conventionally 'political' focus than the neo-Marxists, in that they concentrate on the activity of government itself. This is evident in a concern with: the emergence of the technocratic welfare state; the changing relations between state, parties and electorate; and the rise of 'cultural' forms of governance. However, a number of similarities can be identified between the two perspectives. It was shown how, in terms of understanding the categories of left and right, elements of undermining, reconfiguration and recombining are discernible in the anti-technocratic account. Likewise, each of the four types of relationship between social change and political agency can be inferred.

Consequently, as with the neo-Marxists, anti-technocratic responses to the Third Way fail to elaborate an approach which is both grounded in, but can also politically lead, processes of social change. The neo-Marxists' account emphasised the imperative of capital accumulation driving social and political change. Mirroring this, the central analytical question for the anti-technocrats is whether the rationalising, depoliticising populism they identify amounts to a conscious strategy on the part of elite actors, reflecting definite interests, or is an inevitable response by governors who are as much constrained by technocratic reason as the governed. These issues are pursued further in the assessment in Chapter 7. The present and previous chapters have focused on radical critiques of the Third Way from outside its own parameters; what follows assesses critiques of the Third Way from *within* its own self-proclaimed social democratic tradition.

6
Social Democrats: *The Real Third Way?*

The Third Way and social democracy

The relationship between social democracy and the Third Way is complex, and beset by problems of definition. Social democracy, of course, can lay claim to being the original 'third way' long before Giddens, Blair and New Labour. Since the nineteenth century, social democrats of various incarnations have sought to chart a way between the excesses of both state socialism and *laissez-faire* capitalism. The present Third Way has had a love–hate relationship with the social democratic tradition. On the one hand, glib Third Way criticisms of the 'old left' have lumped together the many versions of social democracy with communism, state socialism, democratic socialism, Eurocommunism and the New Left. But, having written off socialism altogether, the 'first way' that Third Wayers actually engage with and seek to move beyond (with neoliberalism being the second) is the figure of 'old-style social democracy'. This is based on a rather sloppy characterisation of the post-1945 Keynesian welfare state which we explore shortly.

The picture becomes more complicated when, at the same time as using old-style social democracy as a straw man with which to contrast their position, Third Wayers claim *their* version of a social democratic tradition as their own. They suggest that their project *is* modernised social democracy, but without wanting to be entirely associated with it. Giddens' 1998 *The Third Way* was sub-titled *The Renewal of Social Democracy*, but focused very much on a critique of that tradition. By 2001, however, he was locating the Third Way *as* a social democratic

93

project but with the unhelpful proviso that 'As I interpret [social democracy] here, it owes little or nothing to its usage in previous generations.'[1] In 2002 the claim was that, 'The new progressivism stands firmly in the traditions of social democracy – it *is* social democracy, brought up to date and made relevant to a rapidly changing world.'[2] By 2003 matters were no clearer, with Giddens simultaneously claiming that the Third Way 'seeks to transcend' the old left and free market fundamentalism, yet 'is about the modernisation of social democracy'.[3] Blair has shown similar tendencies, pursuing a critique of the 'monolithic' Keynesian welfare state, but increasingly stressing that Third Wayers 'stand in the tradition of revisionist social democracy, applying the values of the centre-left afresh to new circumstances and challenges'.[4] The Third Way has thus slipped between seeing the project as moving *beyond* social democracy, or simply *updating* it. So to understand social democratic responses to the Third Way, we must first acknowledge the interweaving of the two discourses. What follows briefly outlines some of the issues at stake in different definitions of social democracy. Two broad social democratic responses to the Third Way are then identified: 'traditional' and 'modernising', each of which contains a positive and a critical variant. As with our examination of neo-Marxist and anti-technocratic responses, the social democrats' account of contemporary social transformations are identified. They are then analysed in terms of our understanding of left/right and the relations between social change, values and political action. We shall see that social democracy offers spaces for a much more progressive Third Way. However, the historical limitations of the social democratic project – particularly its limited understanding of the cultural aspects of political strategy – mean it is not of itself sufficient for genuine social transformation on progressive terms.

Defining social democracy

The Third Way's ambiguous treatment of social democracy reflects a longer-term problem of defining the social democratic project. In his early appraisal of New Labour, Colin Hay identifies three 'definitional strategies' with regard to social democracy: in the simple Morrisonian terms of 'what social democratic parties do'; against a benchmark of a perceived social democratic heyday; or against an enduring set of social democratic values.[5] However, there are problems with each of these strategies which highlight the general difficulty of defining a social democratic project.

The first definitional strategy – 'what social democratic parties do' – is problematic because of the sheer variety of social democratic practices, reflected in the many, diverse attempts by academics to define them. A typical example is Merkel's schema which identifies market-oriented (UK), market and consensus oriented (Dutch), reformed welfare (Sweden) and statist variants of contemporary social democracy.[6] In a similar vein, Giddens classifies European welfare states as UK (emphasises services, income-dependent benefits), Scandinavian (high tax, universalist and generous services and benefits), Middle European (low social services, high benefits) and Southern systems (similar to Middle European but less comprehensive).[7] It is clearly difficult to talk in universal terms about 'what social democratic governments do'.

The second definitional strategy locates social democracy against a historical benchmark of its post-war 'golden age'. However, this also overestimates the coherence of a social democratic paradigm. Social democracy is typically pragmatic concerning the political means adopted to achieve certain ends. Given this, we cannot try and define social democracy 'for all time' against a set of practices (the golden age) that would have been a pragmatic response to a historically specific situation. In reality, social democrats have *always* been prepared to adopt a range of institutional and policy strategies to pursue their ends.

The third strategy identifies a transhistorical set of social democratic values. Hay suggests that this is the only basis for a genuine historical, comparative analysis of social democratic regimes, for which he lists three defining characteristics: a commitment to redistribution; democratic economic governance of the market via state intervention; and the social protection of citizens' welfare across their life span.[8] However, these criteria are too specific to be seen as either ethical commitments or transhistorical. Different social democratic regimes have similar ethical commitments, but take different views on the areas Hay outlines. Awareness of this problem has led others to adopt an even more generalised definition of social democracy, claiming it is defined by the permanent revision of *means* to meet broadly progressive ends. Thus, in his detailed account of the past and future trajectory of social democracy, Pierson surprisingly settles for the 'catch-all' definition of a commitment to progressive change from *within* the bourgeois political institutions of capitalism:

> what most persuasively identifies social democratic politics is not so much particular policy instruments (however generally these are characterized), perhaps not even policy ambitions (beyond a general disposition to ameliorate some types and levels of inequality), but rather an approach to the political process – above all, a commitment to piecemeal and 'progressive' change through legal-constitutional and generally parliamentary methods.[9]

This raises the question of quite what sort of social democratic movements can realistically exist *outside* of 'legal-constitutional and generally parliamentary methods', especially given social democracy's avowedly non-revolutionary history. So defining social democracy by its values risks over-generalisation. It is precisely this lack of clarity that is exploited by Third Wayers, who are able to claim that they are meeting the broadly 'progressive' *ends* of social democracy, while at the same time pursuing policies (means) that may be anathema to other social democrats. In particular, the normative definition circumvents the question of whether social democracy is concerned with progression towards a genuine alternative to capitalism (at least in its present form), or whether it is essentially a containing project that seeks to ameliorate capitalism's most damaging effects. The position adopted on this fundamental question clearly influences possible social democratic strategies in terms of, for example, the types of political alliances made and the role envisaged for the state (especially with regard to the extent of public ownership). In sum, the combination of the vast political-theoretical space for social democracy, and the different national histories, cultures and institutions which have filtered social democratic projects, account for the diversity of those who define themselves as social democrats.

This brief discussion indicates the pitfalls of making casual references to 'social democracy', or a 'social democratic tradition', in the fashion of both Third Wayers and their critics. However, the generalised model of 'old-style social democracy' invoked by Third Wayers means that it *is* possible to identify the core components of the postwar Keynesian welfare state they reject. On this model, the state plays a key coordinating, and often ownership and direct service delivery role, in the framework of a mixed economy. This is most evident in pursuing Keynesian policies of economic demand management, including corporatist bargaining between the state, business and labour organisations. Economic policies are aimed at full employment and maintaining continuous economic growth. A strong commitment to more egalitarian outcomes is evident in a comprehensive 'cradle to grave' welfare state administering generous benefits.[10] The key sociopolitical foundation of this settlement was a mass, homogenised and unionised male working class – represented by a party of labour and the unions – and a strong link between work and social and political identity.[11]

Social democratic critiques of the Third Way

It is over the continuing salience of this post-war Keynesian welfare state model that many social democrats have joined battle with the Third Way. As Gamble and Wright point out:

> Some of the strongest criticism [of New Labour] has come from self-professed guardians of the social democratic tradition, who believe that certain core ideas such as redistribution, universalist welfare and economic regulation, as well as the link between Labour and the trade unions, cannot be abandoned without abandoning social democracy itself.[12]

The argument from these 'self-professed guardians of the social democratic tradition' tends to be that this tradition is vital to the Third Way, which is devoid of content on its own:

> it soon became clear that, while useful in identifying new territory and opening up new approaches, [Third Way ideas] could only make sense (and avoid rootless vacuity) if they were securely anchored in the social democratic tradition. In other words, the third way had to be about a new social democracy or it was about nothing. It had to be a new social democracy for new times.[13]

Third Wayers themselves seem to have gradually taken on board this view. We have seen that Giddens and Blair have moved from identifying the Third Way as something that is 'beyond' left and right, to presenting it as primarily a project of modernised social democracy. Commentary on the development of the New Labour administration has also increasingly heralded the return of social democracy. Thus, Gamble and Wright approvingly noted that at the end of New Labour's first term in office there was a 'clearly emerging social democratic identity'.[14] Similarly, an excited editorial in *The Observer* heralded Gordon Brown's 2002 budget, which raised revenue through increasing national insurance contributions, as 'the most significant restatement of the British Social democratic tradition for a generation'.[15] Even a scathing critique of Blair from his 'critical friends' at the journal *Renewal* in 2004 suggested that 'With its investment in public services, the government has qualitatively shifted the terms of political debate on to social democratic territory, and has compelled the Tories to follow suit.'[16]

However, just as the theory and history of social democracy is diverse and complex, social democratic criticisms of the Third Way take on different forms. Two broad responses can be identified, each of which has a positive and a critical variant. What we might call traditional social democracy wants to defend a relatively enduring and coherent social democratic model, on the grounds of either values or practices of the types discussed above. *Critical* variants of this position share some similarities with neo-Marxists, who see the Third Way as a smokescreen for neoliberalism; the Third Way is merely a rhetorical device for justifying the abandonment of social democracy.

By contrast, more *positive* traditional social democrats believe that Third Way programmes *are* in essence social democratic, but are being hampered by refusing to be explicit about it. Journalist Andrew Rawnsley notes that '[New Labour] have been social democrats, but social democrats trapped in the closet. Social democrats who, for reasons historical and electoral, rarely dared squeak their true convictions.'[17] Often from what might be called the 'old right' of the Labour Party, the sense here is of frustration with talk of a Third Way. Such approaches like to place New Labour in the long tradition of revisionist labourism. From this perspective, the task of a Labour government is to maintain growth, high levels of employment, well-funded public services and alleviate the inequalities of the market through modest redistribution. It is a measure of the reconfiguration of left and right that a member of the old Labour right, Roy Hattersley, appears as a left-wing critic of New Labour; consistently arguing for 'old-style' tax and spend policies, and balking at the encroachment of the market into the public services. Such individuals are given heart when, for example, taxation re-emerges as a defining difference between Labour and the Conservatives. In the taxation example, New Labour apparently realised that it is politically unsustainable to promise investment in public services without making the case for taxation to fund it. Positive traditional social democrats argue that 'stealth taxes' are not a long-term policy option or sensible politics. They hope that by redrawing the 'real' battle lines over taxation and other traditional social democratic issues, 'hot air' about a Third Way will be ditched.

What can be seen as *modernising* social democratic responses to the Third Way also have positive and critical versions. Given that Third Wayers describe themselves as modernising social democrats, the positive variant often consists of limited self-criticism and reorientation by Third Wayers; it is largely indistinguishable from what we have been treating as the Third Way itself. This approach is typified by the work of *Policy Network*. Founded by Peter Mandelson, this think-tank and organiser for the modernising European centre-left organises high-profile events for those broadly signed up to the Third Way project, while seeking constantly to renew it.[18] By contrast, the more critical modernising social democratic perspective is the most promising for developing genuine alternatives. It is sympathetic to much of what the Third Way identifies, but believes it has been too quick to discard much of the social democratic heritage. This heritage could be adapted to engage with contemporary change and imbue the Third Way with a more progressive substance.

This critical perspective would like to see the Third Way complete the unfinished business of modernising social democracy. Like positive traditional social democratic responses, it wants to see the Third Way being explicit about social democratic themes, particularly egalitarianism. However, unlike traditionalists it does not seek a return to a static social democratic model. The centralising and potentially authoritarian elements of traditional social democracy, which have intensified under New Labour, have led to a proliferation of calls for a social democratic project that is more liberal and pluralist, as well as egalitarian.[19] The key elements of this critical modernising response to the Third Way are exemplified by Paul Thompson's account of how the journal *Renewal* attempts to position itself when monitoring New Labour:

> Ideology and action should be egalitarian – increasing opportunity, redistributing resources and enhancing social inclusion; pluralist – devolving power, working with and learning from other political forces and institutions in civil society; and socially liberal – protecting rights and freedoms wherever possible and promoting policies in tune with the diversity of communities and families.[20]

The natural constituents of this approach are the many who began with high hopes for New Labour's modernising project, but have become disillusioned with its lack of social democratic progress. They are represented in new think-tanks, such as *Catalyst* and *Compass*, that seek to recast New Labour in a more social democratic direction. The perspective reached full expression in the controversial decision by Thompson and the other editors of *Renewal* to launch an all-out assault on New Labour and ask:

> Are we prepared to risk [electoral] defeat or pyrrhic victory with the bogus radicalism and burned out legitimacy of the New Labour project, or can we re-marshal our forces around a genuinely social democratic programme?[21]

Critical, modernising social democratic responses to the Third Way are potentially the most fruitful in terms of offering a reconstruction. However, there is often still the sense, as with their more traditional counterparts, that Labour needs only to return to its 'true' path or 'real' values; there remains a desire to steer Labour towards long-standing social democratic goals. While this is entirely legitimate, it underplays the fact that the Third Way was a response to definite challenges posed by new social and economic conditions. For any critique and reconstruction of Third Way politics to be successful, these new conditions and 'actually existing' Third Way ideas themselves need to be fully engaged with. This will involve calling into question elements of the social democratic 'tradition' itself, and asking if it provides the resources for the kind of proactive politics of social *transformation* that many social democratic critics call for. This question is explored below using the same format applied to the neo-Marxist and anti-technocratic perspectives. The sociological assumptions of social democratic responses to the Third Way are outlined, and the implications for left/right, and the relations between social change and political agency, are then discussed.

Sociological conditions

Chapter 1 showed how the Third Way is predicated on claims that contemporary global conditions have undermined the objectives, the historical agents and the policy instruments of social democracy. Much of the social democratic response sets out to challenge the veracity of such claims. Arguments that social change has undermined left and right, to the extent that social democracy is historically obsolete, are flatly rejected by both traditional and modernising social democrats.[22] Where social democrats do recognise the Third Way's sociological claims, they argue that dramatic social changes do not undermine the viability of distinctly social democratic responses. More boldly, some even argue that social change may even have *increased* the need for specifically social democratic interventions.[23]

Rejecting the straw man of 'old-style' social democracy

First and foremost, social democrats query the Third Way's characterisation of social democracy itself. In the most important defence of this type, Chris Pierson notes how the imaginary of post-1945 social democracy has become almost too embedded in the public mind to allow for a detached analysis:

> Accounts of social democracy in this period have acquired an almost canonical status as the embodiment of what social democracy really is, and this presents a particular problem as we try to think about the ways in which social democracy might now be either 'exhausted' and/or 'reconstructed'.[24]

Pierson suggests, with the accounts of those such as John Gray and Giddens in mind, that it was only with the supposed *passing* of social democracy 'that we find its fullest and most explicit typification', from its *critics* on both right and left rather than its advocates.[25] It was on the back of this retrospective 'straw man' that the necessity of a Third Way was advanced. Against this, social democrats point to the successful performance and ongoing salience of traditional social democracy. The defence is underpinned by the claim that social democracy has *always* drawn on a range of broadly progressive traditions, and was never as dogmatic as Third Way revisionists portray it. As David Marquand argues:

> social democracy is, by nature, heterogeneous. There has never been a single social-democratic orthodoxy, and it would be astonishing if one were to develop in this time of bewildering flux. Now, even more than in previous decades, it is wiser to think of social democracies than of social democracy.[26]

Likewise, Pierson suggests that there is no uniform 'social democratic benchmark' against which subsequent projects can be judged.[27] Rather than being tied to specific political alliances, institutional arrangements and policy tools, social democracy was always pragmatic about the means of delivering its progressive ends – the purveyor of 'what matters is what works' *par excellence*. Social democrats claim that this pragmatism has always been evident – in the forging of cross-class alliances for the purposes of winning elections and building consensus around social democratic policies. In this sense, although social democracy has relied on the (unionised) working class, it has never done so exclusively. As such, even if claims as to the demise of the working class are correct (although these, too, are challenged), it does not follow that social democracy is inevitably consigned to electoral failure.

In terms of policy, social democrats claim that they were never solely reliant on the now supposedly defunct Keynesian economic strategies, or excessively preoccupied with the welfare state in social policy. Contrary to the Third Way charge that old-style social democracy focused on rights at the expense of responsibilities, social democrats claim that they always had a reciprocal conception of the relationship between them. Pierson suggests that 'social democratic welfare policy was always a little more conditional than talk of citizenship rights might seem to suggest', and that 'the idea that one might choose voluntary unemployment and still be supported by the state is quite at odds with the social democratic tradition'.[28]

Finally, the defenders of traditional social democracy challenge the view that it ended in failure amidst the economic and social crises of the 1970s. In the British case, the Labour government had abandoned Keynesian economic management *before* the 'winter of discontent' of 1978–9, with monetarist policies famously introduced by Callaghan in 1976. This implies that the problem of 'ungovernability' identified in the 1970s was one confronted by *all* types of governors, and was not specific to social democrats. On this basis, the same might be said of the contemporary challenges of social change. As Pierson notes:

> If there are no 'special' social democratic problems with demo-graphic change, just those that any governing force would have to confront, this will hardly count as a knock-down argument against confronting the problems using social democratic tools.[29]

The nation-state still has autonomy

Post-war social democracy is typically presented as dependent on the capacity of individual nation-states to pursue domestic social demo-cratic strategies. Economically, this is due to the extent of economic control needed to develop a successful demand-management, Keynesian economic strategy. Politically, the reliance of social demo-cratic parties upon the organised working class has made the mass party form central to social democratic politics. On the Third Way analysis, owing to globalisation, social democracy is held to have declined along with the capacity of the nation-state itself.

Against this, social democrats query the claim that globalisation necessarily undermines the economic autonomy of nation-states. Most fundamentally, Hirst has challenged the extent to which patterns of global trade represent any greater interdependence than at other periods in history.[30] Others, such as Garrett and Vandenbroucke, argue that no matter to what extent trade between nations might increase and intensify, it does not follow that this must lead to a *qualitative* adjustment in terms of domestic economic and social policies.[31] Indeed, Pierson cites evidence to suggest that just as economic globalisation is held to constrain domestic welfare policies, the strength and entrenchment of European welfare states can in fact *constrain* economic globalisation.[32]

Underpinning this is a long-standing debate concerning the degree of national autonomy that can be exercised in the face of constraints imposed by global capital.[33] Social democrats, like some of the neo-Marxists discussed in Chapter 4, challenge the idea that economic globalisation is an external force which diminishes the agency of nation states. However, neo-Marxists often project economic global-isation as a *willed* project, representing definite interests, almost to the point of a conspiracy theory. Alternatively social democrats, while acknowledging the role of interests, tend not to account for globalisation solely in terms of the actions of a capitalist class who must be challenged head-on. Rather, the task is to identify the remaining political space for national, social democratic interven-tions in the face of various economic, social and cultural constraints.

'Reflexivity' and lifestyle changes are exaggerated

Traditional social democrats challenge the cultural effects that Third Wayers suggest follow from globalisation. These include a shift to 'reflexive' lifestyles and 'post-materialist' values (Chapter 1). Third Wayers suggest that 'old-style social democracy' was reliant on a cul-tural formation that has disappeared: a homogenised, deferential working class with a production-oriented identity based on a 'male breadwinner' model. The emergence of reflexive, post-materialist individuals is held to have undermined the cultural base of social democracy. As with globalisation, social democrats query the extent to which greater cultural interaction should represent a qualitative shift of the kind outlined by Giddens and others. Vandenbroucke argues that Giddens fails to demonstrate any *causal* link between the macro processes he identifies, and the concrete problems encountered by social democratic regimes:

> I see no clear link between his [Giddens'] notions of 'intensified social reflexivity' or 'the post-traditional order' and the problems which beset economic policy in the 1980s and 1990s … Giddens' terminology obscures rather than clarifies the problems of social democracy.[34]

Vandenbroucke goes on to suggest that far from the 'golden age' of Keynesian social democracy being characterised by stable lifestyles, it could be argued that 'Keynesian demand expansion was successful in the golden era of social democracy, precisely because western Europe went through a period of rapid and profound change in lifestyles.' Such change was fuelled by the mass consumption of new consumer durables.[35] Vandenbroucke is surely right to challenge the lack of empirical specificity in Giddens' work, and suggests in his theory of expanding consumerism a plausible account of his own. However, although there is no reason to accept the specific social-theoretical constructions of Giddens and others at face value, the social demo-cratic refutation of them represents part of a general refusal to engage with cultural politics. This has hampered social democracy in the past, and continues to do so in its response to the Third Way.

Class continues to matter in politics

Central to the Third Way is an account of class and partisan dealign-ment amongst the electorate, and of the declining political influence of class per se (Chapter 1). This is based on claims about the shrink-ing of the manual working class and the decline of class as a source of identity; evidenced, for example, in falling trade union membership and power. Given that social democracy purported to represent the interests of the working class, supported by organised labour, this is held to represent the demise of social democratic politics.

Like neo-Marxists, social democrats reject these charges on a num-ber of counts. Most fundamentally, they point to the continuing influence of class dynamics in politics. Chapter 4 noted Crouch's claim that while the first half of the twentieth century represented the upward trajectory in economic, social and political power of the working class, we have subsequently witnessed a resurgence of the power of the capitalist class.[36] Similarly, David Marquand charac-terises the (continuing) neoliberal period as a 'capitalist renaissance', akin to the *laissez-faire* conditions of the nineteenth century, with workers more vulnerable and capital stronger than at any point in history.[37] A similar analysis informs Will Hutton's account of the comparatively recent transformation of the 'rules of the game' of cor-porate practice, in which the ruthless pursuit of shareholder value at all costs has become the accepted norm, reflecting the rise and con-solidation of the power of finance capital.[38] The problem of corporate power and accountability that informs all such analysis has come to prominence in the light of evidence of mass accounting scandals occurring in the 1990s.

Against this backdrop, social democrats point to the continuing political significance of social classes. Some simply challenge on empirical grounds claims to the numerical decline of the working class. It is pointed out that global and national social inequalities have increased dramatically since the late 1970s and the ascendancy of neoliberalism; if anything, conflict between capital and labour has intensified.[39] Similarly, the thesis of electoral class and partisan dealignment is notoriously contested among psephologists. Heath *et al.* have claimed that key assumptions made about the British electorate by New Labour modernisers were simply false.[40] As Gamble and Wright argue:

> the electoral success of Thatcherism was not matched by its ability to change the underlying political and social values of the British people. Even when they voted for Mrs. Thatcher, they were not Thatcherised. Instead, they remained stubbornly social democratic in their basic values. What they lacked, in the 1980s, was an effective social democratic party to vote for.[41]

A second type of response acknowledges that the working class has been transformed, but argues that this has not diminished the need for the interests of working people to find political expression. On this basis, Krieger proposes the *re-forging* of the link between working-class identities and social democratic politics.[42] White locates such a project as reflecting the need for a 'cultural politics of post-industrial social democracy':

> Social democracy of the industrial age could rely on a large working class to provide a significant social base for [solidaristic] sentiments. A post-industrial democracy, however, cannot. To a greater extent than before, therefore, social democracy must view these sentiments as a policy *objective*: as something to be consciously cultivated and reinforced within [a class complex] society.[43]

The rationale and content of themes that might inform such a project are pursued in Part III.

Social democrats also illustrate the continuing political salience of class by pointing to the development of an 'overclass'. This is made up of the richest, often internationalised social elites who exclude themselves from the wider society through 'gated communities'. The overclass is characterised by the use of private schooling and healthcare, housing enclaves and a self-imposed isolation in leisure activities. Highlighting the emergence of this group ties together other themes which social democrats believe have been conspicuously overlooked by the Third Way: inequality and the importance of the public realm.

Inequality and the decline of the public realm

Third Way advocates openly claim they are concerned with tackling poverty and exclusion at the poorest end of society, but not the *differential* between rich and poor; as Blair famously put it in 2001, 'It's not a burning ambition for me to make sure that David Beckham earns less money.'[44] Social democrats highlight how a sustained period of neoliberalism has left societies more unequal, domestically and internationally, than ever before. In 2004 the Institute of Public Policy Research published an 'audit of injustice' in the UK, ten years on from its influential *Commission on Social Justice* report for Labour when in opposition.[45] The report flagged up how, despite some progress in certain areas, the yawning gap between rich and poor had continued to grow under New Labour. Social democrats maintain that despite measures to raise the poorest out of poverty, increasing social inequality has corrosive effects upon precisely the social solidarity, or 'community', that is apparently central to the Third Way. Inequality causes resentment and removes elites (and their obligations) out of the mainstream, further fragmenting already fragile capitalist social relations.

The social democratic focus on class dynamics reveals affinities with neo-Marxist critiques. However, in contrast to neo-Marxists, more pluralist social democrats place a particular emphasis on how a return to *laissez-faire* capitalism and increasing inequality is linked to the erosion of the *public realm*. A thriving public sphere is vital to social democratic politics if it is to generate the political will and resources to tackle the inequalities produced by capitalism. In a work devoted to a defence of this idea of the public, and a critique of New Labour's retreat from it, Marquand argues forcefully that 'the public domain is the instrument through which market imperatives are made subordinate to social necessities and social priorities: the means through which markets are mastered for the public good'.[46] Marquand traces how the idea of the public has been assaulted by both centralised state power and free market ideology. Those who defend the public realm in this fashion argue that it is not enough for social democrats to redistribute wealth and opportunity – they must also promote the values of social solidarity and cohesion that flow from, and enable, a more egalitarian and active public culture. Thus, following New Labour's budget of 2002, heralded by Downing Street as 'the last chance for social democracy' because of its raising of national insurance contributions to fund the health service, the *New Statesman* complained that:

> The problem is that the language used to sell higher spending on public services actually undermines social democracy. The public is offered healthcare and education, complete with choice, smooth delivery and value for money, as though they were fast-moving consumer goods. There is nothing here about the public sector's role in creating social solidarity, nor about how the point of its services is to treat people of all incomes and classes equally.[47]

Summary

Social democrats challenge Third Way sociological claims which undermine the historical viability of social democracy. First, the Third Way straw man of 'old-style social democracy' is rejected. Second, it is argued that even if significant economic globalisation is allowed for, the nation-state still has considerable autonomy to pursue social democratic strategies. Third, the cultural and lifestyle changes that are held to follow from globalisation, and undermine the social basis of social democracy, are challenged in terms of their analytical coherence, empirical veracity and their novelty in terms of presenting a threat to social democracy. Fourth, the continuing importance of class politics and the destabilising effects of increasing social inequality are emphasised, as is the corresponding value of collective, public responses. Finally, the boldest claims are that far from undermining the social democratic project, the social changes identified by the Third Way make social democratic strategies more necessary than ever.

Implications for left/right

Elements of the neo-Marxist and anti-technocratic responses to the Third Way *share* its conclusion that left and right are redundant. By contrast, social democrats strongly defend the continuing relevance of the distinction, rejecting Third Way claims that new social conditions have made social democracy obsolete. Thus, the idea of the *undermining* of left and right does not feature in the social democratic analysis. Paradoxically, there is a sense in which this defence of the left/right distinction does undermine the notion of social democracy as a *technocratic*, centrist project. This is largely because, in the face of a Third Way which has adopted the most technocratic elements of social democracy, critical social democrats have been forced to highlight the *values* that make their project distinct from Third Way managerialism.

The subsequent repositioning of social democracy as somewhere on the left of the Third Way represents a *reconfiguration* of left and right. This is particularly the case in the 'rejectionist' strand of social democracy, which adopts a defensive position against the Third Way's attempts to dismantle social democratic achievements, most notably in welfare. For example, Hirst argues that:

> Welfare is the non-optional element in the [social democratic] project, and if it is destined to be cut back to Poor Law standards under international competitive pressures, then the wider agenda of social democratic reform is stalled and the only hope is a dogged defence of what entitlements can be salvaged.[48]

This type of defensive position bears out Giddens' analysis of a political reconfiguration owing to the new 'conservatism of radicals'.[49] On this view, the left (in this case, traditional social democrats) is seen to be anti-modernisation, concerned only with, in Blair's words, 'a hopeless defence of the post-1945 big state in the belief that without big government, a fairer society is impossible to achieve'.[50] This is the battle being constantly played out over welfare modernisation. The conflict is particularly acute in countries such as Germany, where the idea of collective provision has not yet undergone the neoliberal assault it did in the UK. This makes the task for Third Way reformers that much harder, and the divisions with the traditional left even starker.[51]

There is a further reconfiguration of left/right in the potential for a modernising social democratic formation to the *right* of the Third Way. In the Third Way's early days, this seemed hard to imagine. However, as the New Labour project has unfolded it has become clear that the 'ultra-modernisers' – among the New Labour and US New

Democrat elites – are prepared to adopt positions to the right of what even many initial Third Way enthusiasts could contemplate. In the US, following the defeat of Al Gore in the 2000 election, Democrat modernisers such as those associated with the Clintonite Democratic Leadership Council chastised the party for *not being modernising enough*. They proposed not a return to an imagined traditional Democrat orthodoxy, but measures such as the further aggressive targeting of 'Middle America' through economic packages including deeper tax cuts. This represented what can only be regarded as a shift to the right against social democratic criteria. The argument will intensify in the light of George W. Bush's 2004 re-election, as Democrats struggle with how to respond to an apparently conservative US majority. The same line was adopted by New Labour modernisers following electoral setbacks for European social democratic parties in 2002, with calls for the centre-left to take a far tougher approach to crime and immigration issues in particular.[52] Similarly, in seeking to define a possible third term for New Labour, the Blairite agenda has revolved around a radical extension of the idea of consumer choice in public services. It is possible that the increasing isolation experienced by Blair, as his premiership has lengthened, can be accounted for in terms of him developing this hyper-modernising position. Social democratic responses to the Third Way thus have the potential to reconfigure left and right by forcing social democracy either to the left *or* right of the radical centre. In both cases, this is made possible by the enduring social democratic belief in a permanent revision of means enabling dramatic strategic shifts.

The modernising social democratic perspective also allows for the *recombination* of aspects of left and right. This is unsurprising given that it is modernising social democratic thinking which is closest to the Third Way – a project based upon the recombination of conventional categories. However, this is also the type of social democratic response best placed to *challenge* New Labour's Third Way, potentially in the name of a more progressive project that is not merely a restatement of the 'old left'. The recombination lies in an analysis of contemporary social change as the opportunity to complete the modernisation of social democracy, but with a more progressive content than the Third Way. This would involve introducing aspects of both the liberal *and* egalitarian political traditions that are neglected by the Third Way at present.

Assessment: sociological-value relations

In both the neo-Marxist and anti-technocratic critiques of the Third
Way, the functionalist account of the relationship between social
change and political values dominates. However, for social democrats
it is the agency-driven perspectives of updating values, or leading
with enduring values, which stand out. Social democrats reject the
Third Way's claims to being simply a functional response to external
social change; neither the nature of such change, nor possible
responses to it, are seen as fixed and given. Social democrats do not
see their project as merely historically contingent, tied to a particular
set of circumstances – politics *shapes* social change. In particular,
social democrats recognise that the current social and political terrain
was actively fashioned by two decades of neoliberal ideology and politics. Given this, they are critical of versions of the Third Way as an
inevitable, functional response to social change, as this would necessarily make it an accommodation to neoliberalism. The point is illustrated by Labour MP Angela Eagle's critique of the Third Way strategy
of 'triangulation', seeking to split the left/right difference on any
given issue:

> Following a period of right wing ascendancy, to which the centre-
> left will have already accommodated by definition, a tactic of
> triangulation will produce a more right wing solution than would
> otherwise be the case.[53]

The idea of a *historical confluence*, between social democratic values
and contemporary circumstances, is a theme in both traditional and
modernising social democratic responses. At a defensive level, traditionalists suggest social democracy is necessary to repair and guard
against the global inequality and social corrosion caused by neoliberalism. But the most imaginative approaches go on the offensive, and
link social democratic solutions specifically to the themes highlighted by the Third Way. Using the Third Way's 'what matters is
what works' criteria, it is argued that contemporary challenges show
collectivist solutions as the most rational. Will Hutton has consistently argued that the poor state of Britain's public infrastructure, following the neoliberal 'experiment', has convinced the public of the
need for the state to guarantee public goods such as the railways.[54]

Others have suggested that the Third Way challenge of how to provide welfare, in the context of new types of risks and hazards, necessitates collectivist solutions.[55] Thus, only a universalist approach can overcome the pensions 'time bomb', or guarantee long-term health care in an era where genetic testing may exclude millions from private health insurance. At the global level, Michael Jacobs has argued that 'ecological modernisation' requires social democratic strategies, such as corporatist bargaining and an agreed, national and international management plan.[56] With regard to global security and international terrorism, Third Wayers themselves have taken the lead in showing how, in Blair's words, 'A world that is more insecure, needs a political philosophy based on collective security, solidarity and mutual support.'[57] While Blair's closeness to a unilateralist US may have sidelined any social democratic narrative in this regard, there is a growing body of work articulating global governance strategies that ally the social democratic tradition to geopolitical issues.[58]

Modernising social democrats also deploy the *updating values* approach. We have seen that for some, social democracy is defined by the constant updating of broadly progressive values to meet new times. However, modernising social democrats, like Third Wayers, suggest that the extent of social change requires a more fundamental and far-reaching revision of social democratic values. Marquand argues for the *pluralisation* of social democracy, based on his long-standing critique of the statist and technocratic aspects of British labourism. In the conditions of individualisation and social reflexivity described by Giddens (Chapter 1), such calls are given added impetus. Marquand and others agree with the Third Way analysis that contemporary conditions mean that hierarchical, statist, command and control systems are no longer viable. They want the Third Way to follow through this insight more convincingly, with a greater devolution of political decision-making.[59] Related to this, modernising social democrats place more emphasis on the intermediary institutions of civil society than was the case in statist versions of social democracy, and in the contemporary Third Way. These institutions are seen as both a good in themselves, but also specifically as sites from which social democratic parties can learn and revitalise their ideas. Thus, Crouch suggests that 'Democratic politics ... needs a vigorous, chaotic, noisy context of movements and groups', warning that 'For organizations of the political left in particular, denial of the role of identity formation among those outside narrow elite circles constitutes a denial of their own sources of vitality.'[60] Tony Fitzpatrick works these ideas up into a model of 'participative equality', through which he proposes the radicalisation of social democracy against both old left statism and Third Way depoliticisation.[61]

Modernising social democrats have also sought to update their thinking about redistributive justice, and the balance between rights and responsibilities. Clearly, this is another major theme pursued by the Third Way itself. However, social democrats argue that negotiating this balance has *always* been a core concern of social democracy, particularly in the context of ameliorating poverty and providing opportunity. Where the Third Way emphasis is very much upon the obligations of those excluded at the bottom (to find work), social democrats place at least as much emphasis upon the obligations of the (self) excluded at the top. This is in terms of obligations to pay taxes and integrate into the wider society, as opposed to opting out and perpetuating gated communities.

Overall, the most visible social democratic response to the Third Way emphasises the leading role of social-democratic *values*. For traditional social democrats, if the Third Way is to have meaning it must be grounded in an enduring, social democratic, normative tradition which it has thus far neglected. Such a tradition is represented by a set of values prior to and transcending the social changes identified by the Third Way. It is only the *means* that should change – the values remain the same. While this is also the broad claim made by Third Wayers, traditional social democrats are concerned that the Third Way represents more than just a shift in means; the social democratic values themselves have come under threat. Modernising social democrats agree that their project should be value-led, but not necessarily on the 'enduring' terms identified by traditionalists, or those of Third Wayers. With a growing restlessness about the inability of the Third Way to inspire any *depth* of support, both positive and critical modernisers are casting around for the 'right' values with which to capture the public's imagination.

Conclusion

Of all the critics reviewed over the last three chapters, social democrats are obviously ideologically closest to the Third Way itself. They are also the best placed to develop the Third Way agenda. In particular, critical, modernising social democrats come close to the criteria outlined in Chapter 3 for reconstructing the project: acknowledging the significance of social changes, while identifying how a normative agenda can be used to shape them progressively. In contrast to the anti-technocrats and to a lesser extent the neo-Marxists, social democrats identify and vigorously defend a space in which politics can still be conducted in a meaningful way. This is achieved through the defence and sharpening of the categories of left and right. Social democracy is presented as battling on a terrain still dominated by neoliberal assumptions and practices: a struggle between left and right. In addition, the viability of politics per se is expressed through defending the idea of a public realm and collective action for the common good.

Despite this, social democracy by itself does not provide a sufficient response to the challenge presented by Third Way politics. Traditional social democrats compare the Third Way unfavourably to an imagined social democratic benchmark. However, the diverse theoretical and practical history of social democracy shows that no such benchmark exists. Indeed, insisting on a single social democratic standard would give weight to the claim that social democracy is now outdated. In addition, traditional social democrats have failed to appreciate that the Third Way analysis needs to be taken seriously, and social democracy revised accordingly. More affirmative traditional accounts suggest that the Third Way *is* social democratic, despite its unwillingness to acknowledge the fact. However, such approaches fail to note the novelty of Third Way discourse and policy mixes. Much of the Third Way agenda is genuinely at odds with the core themes of social democracy in its many forms.

Modernising social democracy, where it is something distinct from the Third Way, offers a better prospect of a more progressive challenge. It engages with and adds to the Third Way's sociological themes, but tries to approach them in a recognisably social democratic fashion. However, of itself this response is also insufficient. Having identified the new times, modernising social democrats need to create the new constituencies, and narratives, that will lead social changes in a social democratic direction. In short, they require a form of *cultural* politics. This is where, for the moment at least, social democracy comes up short. Previously, 'culture' for social democrats had been assumed: it was either deemed unimportant to a project that delivered technocratic solutions, or was defined as the largely homogenised, working-class identity that sustained social democratic parties at elections. But now it is through cultural interventions that social democracy needs to reinvent itself.

At present, the social democratic response to this cultural deficit is to appeal to an enduring, or reconstructed, set of values. But this is not enough. New progressive values need to be grounded closely in the new world identified by sociological analysis, and show how that world can be steered progressively. Social democracy, with its self-confessed role of ameliorating capitalism *as it is*, is weak on the theoretical and historical resources required to engage in this type of transformative politics. Reviewing the strengths and weaknesses of the critics discussed over the last three chapters, Part III develops a theoretical and political approach that might assist social democrats in developing the cultural resources to move decisively beyond the Third Way.

Part III
After New Labour

7
Developing the Critics

This chapter draws together the main strengths, and seeks to overcome the weaknesses, of the critics discussed in Part II. This amounts to a theoretical framework with which to reconstruct key Third Way themes in Chapter 8. The critics' weaknesses are summarised in terms of their understanding of both the left/right dichotomy, and the wider relationship between social change and political values. However, their ability to link the Third Way to structural conditions and material interests, and their subsequent defence of a left/right distinction through a critique of the market, needs to be maintained. A disparate, 'cultural' critique of the Third Way is outlined as a means of overcoming the limits of more traditional critics. This is rooted in a historical debate concerning how the British Left should respond to Thatcherism, drawing on theories inspired by neo-Gramscian democratic socialism and post-Marxism. The key strength of the cultural critique is that while it recognises the significance of sociological change, it continuously seeks to shape it through progressive political interventions. However, the cultural critique has weaknesses of its own. While its focus upon politically inflecting social change *implies* maintaining the left/right distinction, it does not by itself deliver a distinctively leftist project. The cultural critics' proposals – typically for increased democratisation – are largely *procedural*: they do not advocate a substantive *content* for a new left strategy. Given this, I argue that the cultural critique can be rounded out using the strengths of the more traditional perspectives. The result could be seen as an attempt to steer a theoretical 'third way': drawing on the strengths of both 'materialist' and culturally oriented critiques of New Labour.

The limits of the critics

The review of the Third Way's critics in Part II showed that they either implicitly buy into Third Way claims as to the redundancy of left and right or, alternatively, rely on a static image of the left–right axis. The latter neglects how left and right have been radically transformed and, in any case, are *permanently contested*. Neo-Marxist and anti-technocratic approaches marginalise left and right by subordinating politics to wider, structural imperatives. For neo-Marxists, the Third Way simply reflects the irrelevance of the mainstream left and right, in the sense that both have always been concerned with facilitating capital accumulation. For anti-technocrats, politics, defined as the space in which alternative social futures can be defined, is undermined by the creeping encroachment of technocratic rationality. Thus, although critical of the Third Way in a normative sense, these perspectives reinforce its claims as to the demise of left/right.

The picture becomes complicated when, elsewhere, the critics also *defend* an enduring left/right distinction. In so doing, they neglect the important effects that social change *has* had upon left and right. Thus, even where neo-Marxists acknowledge a dramatically changed social context, their account of the origins of social change (capitalist economic strategies) and consequent political proposals (strengthening of trades unions, defence of existing welfare institutions) are from the standpoint of an idea of 'the left' that is prior to that changed context. This neglects how social change has had real implications for what leftist critique involves, and how it might be realised. A similar difficulty was identified in traditional social democratic critiques which urge centre-left parties to return to their 'true' social democratic path. This underplays both the pragmatism of previous social democratic strategies, and the historically contingent nature of the social democratic model itself. In short, it is insufficient to either reproduce Third Way claims about the end of left and right, or to defend the distinction on *a priori* grounds that neglect changed circumstances.

With regard to the relations between social change and political agency, we have seen that the critics reproduce the four types of relationship identified in the Third Way in Chapter 3: from the most structurally determined to the most agency-centred. None of the critics recognise both the importance of social change *and* the capacity of political interventions to steer it. Underpinning this is a lack of clarity over the relationship between macro social processes, and the opportunities and constraints these present for elite and non-elite actors. This affects how the critics understand the existing Third Way, as well as any possible reconstructions of it. Both neo-Marxist and anti-technocratic approaches are overshadowed by omnipresent structural forces that determine political outcomes, regardless of the agency of individuals and groups. A contradiction emerges when a notion of agency is introduced to explain and challenge these structural imperatives. This is illustrated below, with reference to the critics' accounts of the origins of the *social conditions* underpinning the Third Way, of the construction of the *political subjects* appropriate to such conditions, and of possible *resistance* and alternatives.

Neo-Marxists and anti-technocrats grant a central role to the structural forces of capital accumulation and technocratic rationality respectively. However, elsewhere they invoke the agency of elites in explaining the construction and deployment of those processes. Neo-Marxists (and some social democrats) aim to show how transformations such as globalisation, which the Third Way treats as given, are in fact the outcome of deliberate elite strategies. Indeed, on this account the entire neoliberal dominated, sociological landscape that Third Wayers describe, can be seen as the result of prior normative and ideological *choices* (of the neoliberals themselves).[1] Similarly, we have seen how for some anti-technocrats, depoliticisation is a *deliberate* electoral and governing strategy. The difficulty in both cases is the implication that elite actors are somehow outside or immune from structural changes. The charge of betrayal, which is so often levelled at those who have endorsed Third Way politics, implies that political actors have simply chosen to turn their backs upon a set of socialist or social democratic values, regardless of structural conditions. This account neglects how elites *themselves* have been influenced by the new sociological context.

Critics also grant agency to elites in constructing the political subjects appropriate to these new sociological conditions. Neo-Marxists have pointed to the promotion of flexibility, teamworking and a shift from hierarchies to 'networks' as an *ideological* offensive, aimed at adapting managers and workers to a reconfigured mode of production. Under the guise of moves towards greater empowerment in the workplace, discourses such as 'flexible working' are a functional prerequisite for continued profitability. More directly, the Third Way rhetoric of 'no rights without responsibilities', and a repeated emphasis on the importance of work, is held to be a deliberate strategy aimed at introducing a 'workfare state'.[2] Anti-technocrats extend this approach to describe a new relationship between the governors and the governed, in which individuals are encouraged to internalise state power to the extent that they become self-regulating. Again, such an account drifts towards a conspiracy theory which undermines claims about the imposing structural processes behind the new economy. Moves towards new types of flexible working, and self-regulation generally, are not simply the result of consciously devised elite strategies to con the workforce into adapting to new conditions. The prophets and managers of the information economy buy into the ideology of a 'paradigm shift' in the way we work just as readily as the workers themselves – *they believe their own rhetoric.*

This focus on agency is also evident in accounts of how the Third Way might be resisted. Anti-technocrats, with their rather bleak account of the domination of technocratic reason, have little to say on this front. However, the neo-Marxists continue to seek a version of their long-standing agent for progressive social change: the proletariat. Thus, having surveyed the prospects for oppositional movements just prior to New Labour, Ralph Miliband called for the re-strengthening of organised labour as the main task for socialists.[3] Alternatively, but with a similar end in mind, Callinicos offers an orthodox Marxist critique of the Third Way that looks to the revolutionary potential of the 'anti-globalisers' to challenge capitalist advance.[4] So having identified the determining power of the logic of capital accumulation, it is the *agency* of the modern proletariat that is relied upon to challenge that very same logic. This is despite the fact that the structural processes acknowledged elsewhere by neo-Marxists (e.g. in work and identity formation) have radically diminished, if not destroyed, the revolutionary potential of any (quasi-)proletarian group. In this case, then, too much potential agency is granted to non-elite actors. Social democratic critiques have similar problems in suggesting sites of resistance to the Third Way, but here the emphasis is on the agency of elite or established mainstream actors. For all their moves towards pluralism and subsidiarity, social democrats ultimately rely on either the agency of social democratic *parties* to bring wayward Third Way elites into line, or for those elites themselves to have a change of heart and do the right thing by enacting more social democratic programmes. The latter is the constant hope of unhappy Labour Party members, who mistakenly thought that the whole New Labour enterprise was just a clever piece of marketing to be discarded for a 'real' Labour agenda in government. Again, the changed structural context within which parties and their elites are operating is underplayed.

The strengths of the critics

Despite these problems, this section argues that the Third Way's critics offer two key insights that should inform any reconstructive project: linking Third Way strategies to particular interests or specific material conditions, and conducting a defence of the left/right dichotomy *per se*. While I have argued that a *static* understanding of left/right is inadequate, maintaining the importance of the distinction, in terms of a critique of the commodification of social life, is vital to any new progressive strategy.

A recurrent criticism of the Third Way is that its managerialism ignores structurally embedded relations of power, and the political interests that arise from them. In Third Way sociology, phenomena such as globalisation assume a life of their own, divorced from the interests and strategies of real agents. At the extreme this is evident in what I labelled functionalist Third Way thinking, in which values and policies are seen as determined by external social changes. In the case of Third Way values, 'equal worth' or 'opportunity' are presented as enduring abstractions, with little regard for how they have been determined by their empirical context. Underpinning this tendency is the Third Way urge to synthesise. Third Wayers constantly seek 'win–win' solutions and underplay possibly irreconcilable tensions – between either certain values (e.g. equality and opportunity, fairness and efficiency) or particular material interests (e.g. capital and labour). This leads to an 'end of history' perspective in which, in the alleged absence of major ideological or material conflict, politics becomes the managerial art of 'good governance'. As Fitzpatrick summarises:

> New social democrats [Third Wayers] set out to collapse the conceptual and discursive distinctions between Left and Right, public

and private, etc., but in so doing they have to elide the very real divisions, associations and identities which continue to exist and from which those distinctions derive their salience ... Because new social democrats adopt the *vocabulary* of consensus, they imagine that the *reality* of consensus must follow automatically.[5]

In their different ways, the critical perspectives discussed in Part II challenge these Third Way assumptions, and link the Third Way itself to both structural change and specific interests. In particular, the idea of a post-historical scenario devoid of conflict and unequal power relations is flatly rejected. Commenting on Giddens' notion of a dialogic democracy – a politics free of material conflicts – Anderson suggests that on the contrary:

Politics remains eminently strategic: not an exchange of opinion, but a contest for power. If its rhetoric tends to avoid reference to divisions within the social body – parties nominally appealing to the whole nation – its calculus, as any campaign manager knows, does not.[6]

In contrast to the Third Way's post-historical scenario, neo-Marxists identify the Third Way with technological developments and a major recomposition of capitalism. Their key theoretical move is to reconnect ideas about the development of modernity – or its various elements such as politics, economy and culture – to an analysis of *capitalist* development. For example, Callinicos criticises notions such as 'informational capitalism' and the 'network society' being presented as if they were somehow divorced from the logic of capital accumulation which, he contends, is what continues to drive economic innovation.[7] This focus on enduring capitalist dynamics enables theorising about what *causes* the sociological processes invoked by the Third Way, and avoids their reification. There is thus a vital role for a continuing critique of capitalism *per se* when developing criticisms of and alternatives to the Third Way – and this need not involve Marxian economic reductionism. The strength of the neo-Marxist approach is to integrate an account of capitalist logic (as it constrains both 'owners' and 'workers'), material interests and unequal power relations into the analysis. There is, of course, a danger that explaining the Third Way with an abstraction such as 'capitalist logic' reproduces the Third Way's own functionalism. However, the neo-Marxist critique is made more concrete, and given greater dynamism in terms of identifying specific agents, when the Third Way is presented as expressing particular class interests. This opens up the possibility of identifying countervailing actors, with different interests, who might challenge those driving the Third Way.

Related to this reintroduction of the play of interests into the analysis, the second main strength of the Third Way's critics is where they defend the enduring significance of the left/right dichotomy. To be sure, one of my main objections to the critics was that they reproduce the Third Way's *dismissal* of left and right: in neo-Marxist and anti-technocratic approaches politics in general, and by extension the left/right dichotomy, is largely redundant. However, alongside this depoliticising tendency, the effect of challenging Third Way claims to have transcended conflict is to *repoliticise* the terms of debate and reopen a discussion about left and right.

In the modern era, left and right have encapsulated vastly different, and often internally contradictory, discourses and movements at specific moments.[8] However, the categories can most consistently be identified with the attitude adopted towards liberty and equality – crystallised in arguments about the role of states versus markets. Bobbio's *Left and Right* makes the case for the categories' continuing salience purely in terms of the attitude one takes towards equality, which he depicts as a definitively left objective.[9] Salvati applies similar thinking to the Third Way, arguing that such projects have *always* had to negotiate whether their liberal (more concerned with freedom) or socialist (more concerned with equality) elements will dominate.[10] Critics draw on these tensions in deconstructing Third Way claims to have transcended left and right and, in Bill Clinton's words, to have gone 'beyond the either/or politics that has dominated most of the industrial age'.[11] For example, social democrats challenge the Third Way's self-styled pursuit of both equality *and* meritocracy, believing that the latter necessarily undermines the former.[12] Critics also point to how apparently universal Third Way concepts can take radically different political forms. Thus, Chapter 2 showed how 'community' can imply either the abstract 'nation' or a more concrete, localised entity – both of which can be more or less authoritarian or enabling.

For those who point to the material interests underpinning political projects, 'left' typically represents the collective interests of labour, and 'right' those of capital. This view is evident where neo-Marxists and social democrats claim that the Third Way is a neoliberal project of the right. Far from transcending left/right, the Third Way represents the rightward shift of a permanently contested centre of political gravity, owing to a resurgent capitalist class. We saw how Crouch, for example, analyses social democratic retrenchment (represented by the Third Way) in the context of the reversal of half a century's progress made by the working class and the re-strengthening of capital since the 1970s.[13] On this view, the relative status of left and right is determined by the material interests they embody. The appearance of transcendence simply reflects the fact that rightist social interests have, for the time being, won out. The imprint of this shift in the balance of social forces can be traced across the Third Way's major themes. Thus, the move from stressing equality (implying equality of outcome) to equal worth (implying, at most, 'starting gate' equality), and from discussing poverty to exclusion, is held by critics to represent the abandonment of addressing systemic inequalities through redistributive measures. The 'enabling state' favoured by the Third Way is a retrenchment of comprehensive welfare provision *and* a basis for greater surveillance and regulation of individual activity: combining the worst fears of neo-Marxists and anti-technocrats.

Restating the significance of the left/right distinction opens up a challenge to Third Way technocratic claims, in the context of an ongoing progressive political struggle. Nicos Mouzelis notes that Giddens sees a transcendence of left and right in the shift from an 'emancipatory politics' seeking to overcome exploitation, to a 'life politics' centred largely on questions of identity and lifestyle. But for Mouzelis, even 'life politics' can be seen as part of the struggle for various rights that have historically characterised a left project. These have consisted of civil, political, social and now *cultural* rights: the right to construct one's own life-project.[14] What Mouzelis shows is that the emergence of new cultural political issues, or a 'post-materialist' politics, does not mean the end of the unequal power relations which underpin politics, nor the end of recognisably leftist struggles. More specifically, other defenders of the left/right distinction frame these struggles in terms of an ongoing critique of the market, and its tendency to colonise more and more areas of social life. Even if the left grudgingly accepts that markets are now the 'only game in town', left and right will increasingly be defined by where a line is drawn over the extent to which the market is allowed to encroach upon the public sphere. As Lawson *et al.* argue:

> Social democracy and capitalism cannot be triangulated – more of one means less of the other. The job of social democratic governments is to draw and re-draw the lines between democracy and the market, the individual and the collective, the public and the private. If we give in to the principle of market supremacy then we won't know where or how to draw those lines. Worse still, we end up not knowing that lines have to be drawn at all.[15]

On this account, the active defence and renewal of the public sphere could define a new left project. This is the theme pursued in depth by David Marquand, from a critical social democratic perspective, in his analysis of the decline of the public realm.[16]

So despite the limits of the Third Way's critics, they offer important insights that should inform any reconstructed centre-left project. They highlight, in their various ways, the continuing importance of structural interests and power relations in understanding political strategies. Specifically, they point to the ongoing salience of the dynamics of capitalism, and of the conflict between various actors within it, in driving political change and shaping political values. The persistence of a critique of the commodification of social life illustrates the enduring significance of a left/right distinction. What follows attempts to develop these strengths, and overcome the weaknesses, of critical accounts of the Third Way.

Towards a new framework for critique

This section outlines the emergence of a disparate, 'cultural' critique of the Third Way which avoids the weaknesses of other critical perspectives and provides a framework for alternatives. The approach meets the criteria suggested in Chapter 3 for a successful political strategy: recognising and engaging with social change, but also showing how it can be steered in a more progressive direction. It was influential in debates about the future of the British Left in the 1980s and 1990s, but has been lost sight of by the Third Way and many of its critics. The framework includes aspects of what we might call neo-Gramscian democratic socialism, represented most notably by Stuart

Hall, as well as of the post-Marxism and radical democracy associated with thinkers such as Chantal Mouffe.[17] The cultural critique of the Third Way incorporates a range of other critics of New Labour who may or may not align themselves with these theoretical traditions. The perspective avoids treating either social change, or the values and strategies of agents (elite and otherwise), as fixed and given. On this account it is culture, broadly conceived, that represents the site of mediation between the two problematic poles in Third Way theory: sociological determinism on the one hand, and political voluntarism on the other. Instead, the cultural critique seeks to understand social change precisely in the context of the opportunities it presents for progressive political interventions. The constraints on political action are acknowledged, but politics itself remains irreducibly open-ended, the outcomes always up for grabs.

Nonetheless, the efficacy of the cultural critique is hampered by its underplaying of enduring, structural domination and a reluctance to specify programmatic outcomes. I show how this can be remedied by incorporating the strengths of the more traditional critical left approaches discussed above. This involves recognising the impor-tance of material interests and unequal power relations within capi-talism, and a subsequent defence of the left/right dichotomy via a critique of the market. In particular, a reconstructed approach needs to develop *substantive* (as opposed to just procedural) values, grounded in a critique of unequal power relations and commodification. These should highlight the limits of capitalism in its present form and articulate immanent left alternatives. This synthetic, theoretical exer-cise amounts to a framework for understanding and reconstructing the Third Way, which is then deployed in Chapter 8.

Historical and theoretical contexts

Historical context: 'New Times' and the British Left[18]

Prior to the emergence of New Labour and the Third Way, the 1980s and early 1990s saw an argument within the British Left about how to respond to the increasing dominance of neoliberalism. In Britain, this involved understanding Thatcherism and its implications for the Labour Party. Much of the argument focused on whether Thatcher's success was simply part of the swing of the electoral pendulum, with Labour only requiring 'one more heave' to return to power, or whether

Thatcherism represented a fundamental shift in British society. To respond to such a shift would necessitate a dramatic overhaul of the left's assumptions and strategy. In a seminal set of articles for the journal *Marxism Today*, the sociologist Stuart Hall and others argued that Thatcher and her supporters were indeed reflecting and shaping major social changes. They argued that if the left did not wake up to the novelty of the Thatcher enterprise, and the 'New Times' this represented, it would become marginalised in the face of a neoliberal hegemony.[19] Not only had the material conditions of the post-war social-democratic settlement collapsed, but it was the right who had perceived this collapse and were giving it their own political inflection. In particular, the neoliberals had perceived that the corporatist state had come to be seen as overbearing, and capitalised on this by setting themselves up as the champions of freedom. As well as having an economic programme, the neoliberals were engaged in a hegemonic project at the cultural level to win the 'hearts and minds' of key sectors of the electorate. Marquand, a contributor to the original New Times debates, refers to this as a neoliberal *Kulturkampf* in which, 'In their own eyes, the moral or cultural dimension of their crusade was more important than the economic.'[20] He argues that:

By the mid 1980s [the neoliberals] had embarked on a self-conscious, highly sophisticated and astonishingly radical programme of cultural reconstruction, more far reaching than anything attempted since the days of Oliver Cromwell, and more reminiscent of Gramscian Marxism than of anything in the British conservative tradition.[21]

Hall and the disparate contributors to *Marxism Today* sought to understand both the social changes that were occurring and the extent to which they could be given a *progressive* political content. At the time, the New Times theorists were attacked by many on the left for implicitly celebrating the Thatcher project. Like Giddens' account of a politics beyond left and right, their approach was criticised for positing as inevitable both the social changes it identified, and the neoliberal response. As if to confirm this criticism, a number of the individuals involved in the New Times analysis went on to become key figures in the New Labour modernising project, most notably

Geoff Mulgan, who founded the think-tank *Demos* before directing Blair's Downing Street Policy Unit. The majority, however, have been disappointed by the left's response to the New Times, in the form of New Labour. This is epitomised by Hall's persistent critique of the Blair government; he laments that 'Mrs Thatcher had a Project. Blair's historic project is adjusting us to it.'[22]

To understand why Hall and many of the New Times theorists are dissatisfied with Third Way politics, which is after all a recognition of the need for the left to reinvent itself in the face of social change, we need to examine the theoretical approach that characterised the New Times analysis. The recovery of this approach could provide a framework for overcoming the weaknesses in the critiques of the Third Way discussed in Part II. Despite the criticisms levelled at them, Hall and the New Times theorists maintained that social change represented as much an *opportunity* for the left to shape the social and political landscape as it did a threat to some of its assumptions and practices. There was a space to claim the New Times for democratic socialism. This is in contrast to the Third Way and its critics, where they either see politics as the relatively neutral management of sweeping social forces, or overstate the role of political values regardless of the wider social context.

Theoretical context: neo-Gramscian democratic socialism and post-Marxism

Neo-Gramscians and hegemonic struggle

Hall's ground-breaking analysis of Thatcherism needs to be understood in the context of his theoretical debate with orthodox Marxism, developed through his work in cultural studies. Drawing explicitly on the writings of Gramsci, Hall was dissatisfied with a Marxist view of politics which, when it granted any autonomy to 'the political' at all, tended to see political actors and their projects as pre-formed and representing fixed interests. Rejecting this, Hall saw politics as a struggle over *meaning*, that was enacted at all levels of society. In his words, 'ideology is never the *necessary expression* of a class interest. It is the way certain class interests and other social forces attempt to intervene in the sphere of signification, to articulate or harness it to a particular project, to hegemonize.'[23] Politics is thus an ongoing, strategic exercise of which the visible exercise of state power is just one element. As Finlayson summarises, in the Gramscian analysis:

> Politics extends beyond the narrow realm of the state and govern-
> ment, reaching into and shaping the cultural sphere where our
> everyday perceptions are formed. It is the process of binding
> together and redefining these perceptions, building wider social
> legitimacy for a project of transformation. Politics is not the algo-
> rithmic application of a theory of society, but the open-ended and
> strategic production of collective political identities.[24]

Given this, Hall argued that Thatcherism needed to be understood
not as simply a specific group of actors imposing a radical new
ideology from the level of the state, but as the attempt to articulate a
political project by drawing together a number of elements that *were
already present* in society. Hall claims to think of Thatcherism as 'a
mobilization of shifts that were already going on in the socio-cultural
field. It built a political programme by recruiting political agents out
of that wider field.'[25]

The neo-Gramscian analysis of Thatcherism highlights two key
themes that frame its subsequent engagement with the Third Way.
Firstly, it recognises the need to ally political projects with the leading edge of social change: emergent processes, actors and ideas.
Secondly, the neo-Gramscians understand political strategy as the
construction of coalitions of interest into a hegemonic project, or
the quest to control 'common sense'. The neo-Gramscians thus share
with Third Wayers the recognition that 'Long term, modern, progressive outcomes are only possible by attempting to shape historical
change that is already underway, deep rooted, and that cannot be
reversed.'[26] However, the Third Way's functionalist approach treats
social change as a fixed, external constraint. By contrast, for the neo-
Gramscians, social changes are never immutable: they can always be
given a discursive content, or inflection, that leads them in a particular direction. This was exemplified by Thatcherism's appropriation of
the process of increasing individualisation, which it linked to a
neoliberal discourse of individual freedom and opportunity. Finlayson
points out that these divergent views about the character of social
change were evident *within* the original analysis of *Marxism Today*, of
which Hall and others were a part. He suggests that 'The Gramscians
sought to reformulate analysis of the agents that could form a

coalition to bring about social change and the ethico-political basis which would legitimate it. What we might call the "Demos tendency" developed a kind of vanguardist futurism.'[27] It was this latter approach which ultimately informed the Third Way and its sociologically reductionist 'there is no alternative' rhetoric.

The second key theme in the neo-Gramscian analysis is an emphasis upon the development of political agents, and the construction of coalitions, in contrast to the 'vanguardist futurism' of functional approaches. Hall and others criticised the orthodox left for attempting to read off political identities from class location. This led to the complacent view of the 'untapped majority' that Labour simply needed to access. But on the neo-Gramscian view, political identities are never fully formed. To be sure, there are definite material interests within a given society; but for such interests to be politically articulated requires the intervention of politics itself. Political agents need to be constructed and co-opted to hegemonic projects, defined by Gilbert as:

> what you get when one group in society sets out to convince a number of other groups that their interests will be well served by entering into a social coalition in which the hegemonic group is the leading partner.[28]

Hall points to how the Thatcherite political subject was not mechanically produced by the rise of an affluent section of the working class. The political skill of Thatcherism lay in convincing that emerging group that its best interests lay in entering into a coalition with the hegemonic group: in this case finance capital and its political representatives, the Conservative Party. Thus the restricted, short-term interests of a particular fraction of capital were presented as the *universal interest* under the banners of enterprise, freedom and opportunity. These leitmotifs infiltrated public discourse to the extent that they became the new common sense – hegemonic politics *par excellence.*[29] Indeed, it was the governing class in particular who bought into this new mindset, as Marquand observes, 'Neoliberal political economy has become part of the mental furniture of the political elite.'[30]

From this distinctive theoretical approach, the political task for the cultural critics of the Third Way is twofold. First, to identify those elements of social change that represent the leading edge of modernisation. Second, to develop a narrative that might inflect that leading edge in a more progressive direction. In so doing, they need to attract a disparate range of social elements into a *coalition* as part of a hegemonic (or counter-hegemonic) project, in order to achieve a new common sense. For the New Times theorists, not perceiving this task was Labour's downfall in the 1980s when it 'stopped trying to explain the nature of the social and political world to potential voters', in a way which would have provided the necessary 'template through which people interpret their own experiences and desires'.[31]

The neo-Gramscian analysis leads to an automatic rejection of claims to 'the end of ideology' or the 'end of politics', of the sort implied by the Third Way. Politics is *necessarily* an ideological struggle, and the Third Way's narrative of the end of left and right is in fact a highly *political* strategy. Attempting to make the ideological appear as non-ideological is what defines hegemonic politics. This view of the irreducibility of politics is pursued by the second key theoretical influence in the cultural critique of the Third Way: the Post-Marxism most famously expounded by Ernesto Laclau and Chantal Mouffe.

Post-Marxists and antagonism

Post-Marxism emerged out of an extensive and complex theoretical debate.[32] To understand its significance to a critique of the Third Way, three core themes can be highlighted: a *relational* view of identity formation; a subsequent conception of the irreducibility of social *antagonism*; and the advocacy of a *radical democracy* as the appropriate political form to match this ontology.[33] These theoretical assumptions lead to a critique of the Third Way's attempt to both eradicate antagonism and to imply that history, in the form of ideological struggle, is over.

The post-Marxist analysis begins from an account of the *relational* nature of identity. On this view, the identity of an object is never intrinsic, but is always constituted in relation to an 'other' or outside. However, the presence of the external other prevents the initial object's identity from ever being fully constituted. The paradoxical result is that the other is the precondition of, but also the inevitable obstacle to, the realisation of identity. The effect of this ontology is to politicise all social relations:

> It is not that social objects enter the arena of the political with fixed and essential identity and only then confront each other. Instead, the identity of each is forged in 'its' very relations to

diverse others. The construction of social identity is always already political.[34]

The constant relational tension between objects, as both the precondition of and obstacle to identity realisation, means that social life is irreducibly *antagonistic*. Antagonism is the natural relationship between objects (always unsuccessfully) attempting to realise their identity. Given this, politics, and indeed history, is permanently open-ended and contested; political struggle is forever, with no possibility of a *telos* in which antagonism might come to an end. It is only a short step from these theoretical premises to a critique of the Third Way, with its claims to have reconciled opposed interests and found 'win–win' scenarios out of previously conflictual situations – epitomised by talk of being beyond left and right. In the post-Marxist analysis, a single 'complete' position such as the Third Way, which is beyond antagonism, is *ontologically impossible*. The Third Way must have an outside or other, as with all social and political objects. Post-Marxists previously criticised orthodox Marxism's quest for historical closure in the form of communism. Now, the ironic similarity between Marxism's historical stagism and that of the Third Way is noted; Finlayson identifies in the Third Way 'a certain vulgar Marxist tendency, in that it regards itself as in line with a given logic external to its own political interventions'.[35] Post-Marxists are thus critical of the Third Way's implicit sense of historical closure, and its general inability to imagine alternative social futures.

The model of politics that accepts the irreducibly antagonistic nature of social life is a 'radical democracy'. Mouffe seeks a political arrangement that facilitates a move from antagonism to 'agonism' – the reasonable coexistence of the many competing others – so that they might tolerate rather than seek to assert themselves over or obliterate one another. Such a perspective is clearly democratic, in that it focuses on diversity and seeks a set of arrangements to facilitate it. However, there is little in the idea of tolerating multiple, contingent identities that would offend simple liberal pluralism. So what is it that makes radical democracy *radical*? Advocates point to a number of areas. Firstly, because of their politicised ontology of social relations, radical democrats see the potential for absolutism that exists at *all* levels of social life, and not just in the narrow confines of the traditional liberal political sphere. This necessitates strategies for democratisation across social domains, for example in work and the family. Secondly, for radical democrats, in contrast to liberal pluralists, the rules of the political game will only ever be *partially* complete. Owing to their analysis of the always contingent and incomplete nature of political identities, radical democrats see that political settlements can always be subverted and reconstituted. This is because they will have been based on the (only temporary) exclusion of a constitutive other.[36] Such a position keeps the prospect of alternative, more progressive political arrangements permanently alive. Thirdly, and most debatably, radical democrats claim that as they see unequal power relations as constitutive of politics, not only do they expose Third Way claims to have obliterated such relations as impossible, but their position:

> suggests the need for a political approach based upon a radical reassessment of the methods by which power resources are allocated within every sphere of life, as well as a need for a radical shift towards pluralism in lifestyle and behaviour.[37]

That is, the boldest radical democrat claim – about what distinguishes it from liberal pluralism – is that its ontology necessarily points towards greater *equality* in the distribution of power and resources.

The theory of radical democracy certainly leads to a strategy of extending and deepening democracy across social life. In contrast to orthodox Marxists, radical democrats do not regard democracy, and politics more generally, as a mere epiphenomenal reflection of antagonism in the economic sphere. Democracy *itself* is seen as having strongly progressive potential, as summarised by Mouffe:

> The problem with 'actually existing' liberal democracies is not their ideals, but the fact that those ideals are not put into practice. So the task for the left is not to reject these ideals, with the old argument that they are a sham or a cover for capitalist domination, but to fight for their implementation.[38]

Radical democrats offer a compelling critique of the Third Way. But can radical democracy itself form the basis of an alternative, more progressive project? Tying together the strengths of the critical perspectives discussed here, a theoretical basis for such a project is outlined below. This is then used to inform the progressive reconstruction of Third Way themes in Chapter 8.

Towards a reconstructed Third Way

The problems with the critiques of the Third Way discussed in Part II were identified as either the neglect – or a static conception of – left/right, and an approach to social change and political agency that mirrors the Third Way, therefore hampering the development of alternatives. The cultural critique represents an improvement in each of these areas. Firstly, it sharpens our sense of permanently contested left/right categories. Secondly, it has an entirely different conception of the relationship between social change, values and political agency, avoiding both structural determinism and political voluntarism.

From the cultural perspective, neither social processes such as globalisation, nor the agents who construct and are affected by these processes, are immutable. Both social change, and the identity of social agents, are seen as open-ended and subject to political intervention. This is evidenced in the neo-Gramscian concern with inflecting the leading edge of social change, as well as the post-Marxist relational view of identities as never fully realised. The categories of left and right are not static, pre-formed and waiting to be deployed: they have to be given a particular content which itself is not permanent. The cultural critique has vigorously defended the left/right distinction against Third Way claims that it is redundant. In particular, cultural critics have challenged the rise of managerialism in politics as a strategy of *depoliticisation*, in the same vein as the anti-technocratic perspective discussed in Chapter 5. Unlike that perspective, however, the cultural critique sees projects such as the Third Way as sites of permanent contestation which can be steered in alternative directions, rather than as the inevitable, technocratic logic of late modernity. This view is rooted in both the neo-Gramscian and post-Marxist forms of the cultural approach. In addition, the cultural perspective's focus on the constitutive nature of antagonism, and the impossibility of political closure, automatically rejects Third Way attempts to flatten out antagonisms and present itself as a *telos*.

The key political task for the cultural critique is the construction of coalitions in the bid for hegemony. In the neo-Gramscian analysis, politics is the search for the control of 'common sense', by aligning the leading edge of social change with ideological positions. Similarly, in the post-Marxist approach, politics is the quest to (always provisionally) inflect contingent and open-ended subjectivities. Indeed, post-Marxists have a specific view of the political identity they believe it is the task of progressive politics to construct: the radical democratic citizen, able to translate antagonism into agonism (coexistence) in the context of a tolerant, pluralist polity. This bid to hegemonise unites the neo-Gramscian and post-Marxist elements of the cultural critique, and represents both its greatest asset *and* where it would benefit from incorporating the strengths of more traditional left perspectives.

The cultural critique shows that the site of hegemonic strategies, which can broadly be understood as 'culture' or the realm of the 'discursive', represents the *mediating* level between the problematic poles of structural determinism and political voluntarism which we have encountered throughout. It is at this level that the character of social change and the identities of agents are articulated, and coalitions of interest constructed. However, the focus of cultural critics on articulating discursive themes also highlights two key problems for developing a left reconstruction of the Third Way. The first is ontological, stemming from the open-ended character of identities and social change, and the resulting concern with discourse. In traditional left critiques, political projects are linked to material interests and enduring forms of domination and exploitation. By contrast, the cultural approach privileges discourse, and its contingent and open-ended character. This weakens the possibility of identifying 'culture' itself, and political projects such as the Third Way, as embodying recursive forms of domination. As Wood observes in a discussion of Stuart Hall's work on hegemony:

> Discourse theory ... implies identities so frail that they can be 'won' only fleetingly. Such analyses fail to understand meaning as *enduring* domination; they fail to grasp what makes ideology worth studying in the first place.[39]

In particular, in terms of developing a distinctively *left* project, a discourse-centric view makes it difficult to locate meaning as an ideological effect of the *market* form, and the concrete interests that embody it. It becomes difficult to advance a critique of market relations on this basis.

The second, related problem with the cultural critique is its lack of advocacy of a *content* for its project, again so that it might be recognisably of the left. Historically, left projects have advocated a particular type of society and subject – they have had a *goal*. However, the *indeterminacy* of the cultural perspective steers it away from such a vision, in terms of both the structures of a future society, and the worldviews of the individuals who would inhabit it. Hall himself has criticised Laclau and Mouffe in this respect, suggesting that seeing identities as always open-ended and in flux neglects that subjects can actually be 'won over' to a new understanding of themselves and society.[40] The thematic that cultural critics *do* argue for is that of democratisation in general, and a 'radical democracy' in particular. But this project of democratisation is largely *procedural*, and could as easily be adopted by the political right as the left. Again, for a democratising project to have a distinctly left character, the substantive content of the democratic society, and the orientations of the individuals who inhabit it, needs to be addressed. This necessitates consideration of the relationship of democracy to the wider environment of a market economy/society, and the types of individuals it produces.

The cultural critique of the Third Way would thus benefit from incorporating the strengths of more traditional left approaches. A focus on material interests, unequal power relations and enduring forms of domination necessarily leads to a critique of market relations. This critique in turn becomes the focus for maintaining the left/right distinction. By incorporating these traditional left concerns, the cultural critique can link its discursive themes to particular sets of interests, the types of social institutions sought by a left project, and the values required to sustain them. The final chapter develops this approach through a reconstruction of core Third Way themes.

8
Reconstructing the Third Way

Books of this type are vulnerable to the charge of being all about critique, parasitic on existing perspectives and offering no constructive suggestions. Alternatively, whenever closing chapters do put forward tentative proposals, they often feel trite, unoriginal or highly speculative. Wary of these dangers, having analysed the claims of both the Third Way *and* its critics, and sketched out an alternative way of thinking about centre-left strategies, in this chapter I do move to a more reconstructive agenda. But with important caveats. First, it will have been clear that this is not a work of policy analysis, and what follows is certainly not a list of policy recommendations. Second, there is no manifesto here, nor a rallying call to a particular group of agents to enact a political project. Instead, what follows attempts to use the theoretical approach developed over the book to show how key Third Way themes might be reconstructed along more progressive lines. It is hoped that this will suggest the potential for the Third Way to be opened out into different political directions – both within the still unfolding New Labour project and, ultimately, beyond it.

The cultural critique of the Third Way, outlined in the previous chapter, was shown to be useful in viewing social change as open-ended and always subject to political intervention: social life is irreducibly political. On this view it is possible to identify, and give a political inflection to, contested discursive themes. Such themes mediate between describing processes of social change, and giving them a definite political content and direction. However, it was also suggested that the cultural critique could be given a more distinctively left character. This would be achieved by recognising the continuing influence of material interests and power relations upon political forms. Such an approach opens up a critique of commodification and points to the enduring significance of the categories of left and right. In what follows, three interrelated Third Way themes are reconstructed on this basis: individualisation, community and modernisation. In each case, the conservative function of the theme in the current Third Way is reiterated, its more progressive *potential* in current critical accounts is assessed, and an alternative reading with a more distinctly left character is offered. Each example shows that, while the Third Way may have tapped into the main social currents of our time, these could still be rearticulated by a more progressive project of the left. This may have more chance of inspiring support and achieving the kind of lasting progressive consensus that New Labour seeks as its legacy.

Individualisation: from atomism to autonomy

Chapter 1 revealed how the perception of a shift to a more individualised society plays a central role in the Third Way. It is shown below how an atomised, neoliberal variant of individualisation dominates in Third Way thought; this emphasises work, material acquisition and a socially conservative set of responsibilities. New Labour has skilfully plugged into the contemporary desire for individual autonomy in a way that, as Jeremy Gilbert notes, gives its particular version of competitive individualism a 'dangerous resonance with contemporary culture'.[1] Despite this, I argue that there is a richer, more developmental understanding of individualisation to be found, ironically, within the social theory of Giddens. However, if this more progressive version is to be realised, it needs to be supplemented with the more traditional left concerns of addressing unequal power relations and challenging some of the basic objectives of capitalism. The discourse framing the 'knowledge economy' is offered as an example of how an alternative approach might unfold.

The Third Way's conservative individualism

Third Way rhetoric is censorious of certain forms of self-directed behaviour, which it attributes to flaws in both the old left (excessive demands for rights at the expense of responsibilities) and the New

Right (economic greed above all else). It is on this basis that the Third Way talks of 'no rights without responsibilities', and is attracted to the types of institutions that might *enforce* appropriate behaviour. However, beyond this negative definition, the figure of the individual that actually underpins the Third Way in practice is a variant of the economically instrumental, utility maximiser of neoliberalism. Thus, as the New Labour project has developed, much criticism has come to focus on the aggressive attempt to reconstruct citizens as consumers in all spheres of social life.[2] In the same vein, Third Wayers have capitulated to the idea of unlimited consumption as being a defining component of the new individualism. This is most obvious where New Labour politicians (most notoriously Peter Mandelson) have actively promoted and celebrated extreme individual wealth, in one of the most noticeable rhetorical departures from the old left. Over time, the figure of the acquisitive, materialistic consumer has *hardened* in New Labour rhetoric; Blair set out 'aspiration' as the theme that would underpin New Labour's 2005 election campaign, claiming that 'The purpose of New Labour is to encourage personal prosperity and well-being.'[3] This culminated in the stark promise to make 'Your family better off' the leading promise on the party's election pledge card. We are thus curiously left with the promotion of an economically instrumental view of individualisation, or *individualism*, coupled with disapproval of the 'selfish' behaviour that arises as a result. Politically, the paradox is a continuation of the fundamental tension that underpinned Thatcherism. This arises from the desire to maximise individual liberty, defined in economically instrumental terms, but also to bemoan the corrosive effect that an unhampered free market has upon the social fabric.

Reconstructing individualisation

The one-dimensional, neoliberal version of the new individualism is not the only one on offer. The political task for the left is to show how it is only through a more progressive politics that individuals can, in fact, flourish. Interestingly, Giddens' earlier Third Way work points towards such a model. For Giddens and other sociologists, individualisation is presented as the end-product of a series of inter-related social transformations (Chapter 1). On this account, a world of increasing interdependence and instantaneous communication flows is characterised by a 'global cosmopolitanism' which produces more critical, reflexive individuals. This creates a climate of detraditionalisation in which institutions and practices can no longer justify themselves with reference to traditional means, such as arguments of the 'it's legitimate because it's there' variety. Instead, they are forced into a dialogic relationship in which they must justify themselves on the basis of reasoned argument. This leads Giddens to a definition of fundamentalism as traditions which refuse such dialogue and defend themselves self-referentially, or 'in the traditional way'. Individualisation is the result of the loosening of structure wrought by this process of detraditionalisation, through which identity becomes a matter of active self-creation.[4]

We have seen that, in Third Way rhetoric, there is concern that the resulting decline of deference is manifested as selfishness and a lack of respect for social institutions per se. However, while Giddens is certainly alert to this problem, his account of detraditionalisation opens up a more positive agenda, with radical implications that should appeal to progressives.[5] Detraditionalisation implies a decline in arbitrary power and claims to expertise that shroud vested interests. The individualisation that follows suggests people could have greater self-determination than traditional constraints (for example, rigid class structures) have allowed. Giddens' model of the 'post-traditional individual' appears to meet much of what various left projects have traditionally aimed for.[6] Giddens' individual is a creative, reflective figure able to develop unencumbered by the distortions of entrenched, arbitrary interests and domination and exploitation of various kinds. There is thus a gap between the active and reflective citizen operating in Giddens' dialogic democracy, and the atomised, consumerist (yet duty bound) individual in New Labour's Third Way. Driver and Martell observe that 'In this respect, third way ideas can be divided between "post-traditionalists" like Giddens and "social moralists" like Blair.'[7]

The New Times theorists discussed in Chapter 7 were the first to point to how the dynamic of aspiration, opportunity and possibilities for self re-invention, unleashed aggressively by Thatcherism, were a potent political force. This tapped into the broader process of individualisation in the context of a decline of tradition and hierarchy. As Rustin, a critic of possessive individualism, concedes:

> The ideology of individual rights, so actively promoted as a form
> of possessive individualism by the Thatcherites, has undermined

structures of deference and status in ways that could even have some democratic benefit.[8]

The long-term process of increasing individualisation, coupled with the entrenchment of individualist neoliberal ideology, has made it a political non-starter to ever appear to be 'anti-individual' or 'anti-aspiration'. New Labour modernisers have been acutely aware of this: they recall, for example, how such labels stuck with Labour when it opposed plans to enable council house tenants to buy their properties in the 1980s. A reconstructed notion of individualisation thus needs to retain a sense of dynamism and alliance with people's desire for upward mobility. The Third Way has largely sought to achieve this by accepting a model of atomised consumerism. However, if individualisation is to assume a left character, it needs to be uncoupled from this one-dimensional understanding of individual development.

Giddens' model of the reflective citizen in a dialogic democracy shows some promise towards this objective, but is insufficient by itself. It is here that more traditional left concerns come back to the fore. The problem with Giddens' account is that his reflective citizen is not presented as an ideal that the Third Way should strive for, but as the *already existing basis* for Third Way politics. The 'dialogic space' that Giddens' post-traditional individual inhabits is devoid of conflicts of interest, dominant values and unequal power relations. In a context where these distortions remain prevalent, there is a role for the left to address them if Giddens' model is to be at all realisable. A more traditional left analysis is necessary to show where unequal economic and social relations prevent the more developmental individual from taking shape.

The Third Way vision of the knowledge economy illustrates how a reconstructed understanding of individualisation might incorporate more traditional left concerns. Individualisation is held implicitly to be both the cause and effect of the knowledge economy. On the one hand, it is the market for knowledge products and demands for more autonomous and fulfilling types of work – created by an increasingly reflexive citizenry – which is supposed to underpin a shift to a new knowledge economy. In this sense, individualisation is a *cause* of the economic transition. Simultaneously, however, the alleged move to a knowledge-based, flexible and less hierarchical mode of production is also presented as intensifying the process of individualisation itself.

On this account, individualisation is a necessary process of *adaptation* to a new type of economy. This is the focus of much of the anti-technocratic critique of the Third Way described in Chapter 5. Optimists about the knowledge economy point to its capacity to enhance individual autonomy.[9] The decline of command-and-control forms of hierarchical decision-making, and the emergence of horizontal or network-based organisational structures, are held to enable individuals to assume greater control over the work process.[10] In addition, multi-tasking, portfolio working and the time that flexible working frees up for other pursuits are seen as a basis for greater individual creativity. This optimistic account resonates with Giddens' notion of a more progressive, developmental individualisation.

Through a more *critical* appraisal of these developments we can see how the discourse of individualisation might be more clearly claimed by the left. The first task is to recognise that the character of the knowledge economy is not immutable. Even the most ardent promoters of the 'knowledge revolution' recognise how political decisions define its parameters and character. Thus, hyper-modernisers criticise New Labour for over-relying on centralised control mechanisms, rather than developing more devolved and flexible systems appropriate to a knowledge economy.[11] This implies that there is political control – *choice* – over the character of the new economy, in contrast to accounts of the *inevitable* decline of command and control under the pressure of detraditionalisation. Once we accept the role of political choices in this way, a critique of the knowledge economy's content and form can be opened up. In particular, we no longer have to accept its instrumental orientation, stemming from its relationship to an enduring capitalist mode of production. We then become free to consider alternative visions of what constitutes meaningful and fulfilling work in the 'information age'.

At present, this possibility of a more progressive individualisation is threatened by twin pressures. On the one hand, the *form* of the knowledge economy (flexibility, networks, horizontal organisation) is deployed as an external imperative that workers must adapt to. In this sense it is a disciplinary tool (for capital to discipline workers, and the state to discipline both capital and workers) reminiscent of that depicted by the anti-technocrats in Chapter 5. More fundamentally, the *content* of the knowledge economy appears as simply an intensification of long-standing capitalist relations and objectives.

The 'new' knowledge worker still predominantly serves capital accumulation. Even public sector workers find themselves doing so to an
unprecedented extent, with New Labour's encouragement of private
interests into public provision.[12] Furthermore, consumerist ideology
frames the aspirations of individual workers themselves, in the form
of the instrumentalist attitude towards work and consumption promoted by the Third Way. This prioritises material acquisition by 'hard
working families' above the kind of developmental existence implied
by Giddens' reflexive, dialogic citizen.

The knowledge economy highlights the role for more traditional
left approaches in reconstructing individualisation. The new approach
would differ from the Third Way by challenging the deployment of
new technologies and organisational practices purely in terms of a
narrowly defined criterion of capitalist efficiency. It would also challenge the dominant acquisitive and instrumentalist view of individual development. Politically, this suggests an agenda of developing the
knowledge economy towards greater worker control over processes
and outcomes – a very 'old left' objective. It also means embracing
individual objectives that fall outside the instrumental, consumerist
paradigm. These themes are already evident in increasingly urgent
and widespread debates over issues such as the value of care work, the
work–life balance and developing more sophisticated, quality of life
indicators in our understanding of what constitutes economic growth.
Vitally, for a more progressive vision of individualisation to be realisable, a critique of the role of the market in framing the content of
the knowledge economy needs to be maintained. If the Third Way is
to move beyond its atomised account of human agency, it needs to
identify the individual flourishing in the context of *socially oriented*
objectives. It is shown below how reconstructing another Third Way
theme, community, might provide such a context: autonomy is only
achievable for all when backed up by collective action to overcome
the barriers to its fulfilment.

Community: from imposition to empowerment

It was noted in Chapter 2 that community is perhaps the most widely
invoked Third Way value, with critics claiming that it has been
stretched to the point of vacuity.[13] Despite the 'feelgood' quality of
community, the Third Way's strategic use of the concept amounts to

an instrumental vision of economic modernisation, reinforced by cultural conservatism. The latter emerges out of New Labour electoral strategy, which conflates the perceived worldview of an imagined middle class with a universal 'community'. Community is thus a vehicle for imposing values of work-centrism, consumerism and socially conservative understandings of normal behaviour.

Despite this, reconstructing community could facilitate the shift from a neoliberal to a more progressive sense of individualisation. Two strands of thought about the progressive potential of community are examined below. Radical democratic approaches, drawing on the perspective outlined in Chapter 7, seek to manage the inevitable antagonisms between communities. A more defensive, social democratic strategy seeks to protect cultural spaces in which a more solidaristic sense of community might be developed. However, as in the case of individualisation, these alternatives need to be supplemented with more traditional left themes. This involves addressing the structural obstacles to including all sections of the community, and using political leadership to argue for solidarity and empowerment in contrast to the 'neutral' community of simple liberal pluralism.

The Third Way's conservative community of 'Middle England'

The Third Way invokes different forms of community, including a concrete, localised version and a more abstract sense of national belonging. While in theory each of these can be more or less conservative or progressive, New Labour has adopted a deeply conservative version. The Third Way's view of community and the individual is a reciprocal one, as outlined by Finlayson:

> New Labour's vision of the ideal subject is that of the reflexive individual who regards his/her self as a form of capital to be processed, refined and invested, and who does this within the context of an obligation to the community to be productive. Being so will contribute to that community, which in turn contributes to the well-being and prospects for self-capitalisation of that individual. Naturally the whole is contained within the all-embracing economy.[14]

On this view, community is a key term in the Third Way bid to 'economise' all areas of social life, by extending the reach of neoliberal criteria for economic efficiency. While this account illuminates the economic function of community, it is less helpful in explaining the *cultural* conservatism of the Third Way understanding of the term. After all, neoliberal economics could theoretically be complemented with *libertarian* social policy, a path being suggested by some modernisers within the Conservative Party as a way of challenging New Labour 'nanny statism'. In order to understand this cultural conservatism, account needs to be taken of Third Way – and in particular New Labour – electoral strategy.

The social conservatism of the Third Way community results from its conflation with the imagined worldview of a very particular psephological construct: Middle England. Stuart Hall identifies this imaginary as the direct descendant of that upon which the 'authoritarian populism', which he identified as characterising Thatcherism, was based.[15] New Labour pollster and strategist Philip Gould, in his account of the 'unfinished revolution' of New Labour, is explicit that it is the aspirations of this imagined demographic that should determine centre-left strategies. This also illustrates the direct influence of US Democrat strategy upon New Labour. Gould admiringly cites his New Democrat counterpart, Stan Greenberg, for winning the argument in the Democratic Party as to the centrality of the middle class to any centre-left strategy. That this would result in a more culturally conservative politics is immediately apparent. Thus, Gould cites Greenberg's claim that 'To reach the middle class today Democrats need to accommodate "middle-class consciousness", containing three primary and interconnected principles: work, reward for work, and restraint.'[16] Gould insists upon the 'caring' character of this decisive middle-class demographic, and presents it as the starting point for a broader political coalition to include the poor.[17] However, it is the rather less caring elements of this imaginary that are pointed to – Gould lists them as 'hard-working, anxious, ambitious', with an emphasis upon work, consumption and 'getting on'.[18] This cultural conservatism frames the ideal-type of 'community' that New Labour invokes in pointing to individual responsibilities. As with the image of the individualised consumer discussed above, this theme has hardened with the development of New Labour in government. Election chief Alan Milburn opened the 2005 campaign by telling 'hard working people' that 'if you play by the rules, you get a chance to progress'.[19] Happily for Third Way strategists, these values tailor perfectly with the wider project of the neoliberal marketisation of society.[20]

Putting an imagined, culturally conservative Middle England at the centre of party strategy is a pure form of what Colin Hay refers to as 'preference-accommodating', rather than 'preference-shaping', politics.[21] It represents a refusal to use political leadership to try and inflect the preferences of the electorate in a progressive direction. Tom Bentley, director of *Demos* and an advocate of the progressive potential of consumer identities, goes some way to acknowledging this when he notes that 'By accepting the premise that "getting on" in today's consumer society is the main criterion by which citizens will assess how well government is helping them, politics has reduced its own capacity to question and influence the ways in which aspirations themselves are formed and shaped.'[22] The US example is instructive here. With their conservative appeal to the values of Middle America during and after the Clinton years, the New Democrats still failed to prevent the mobilisation in 2004 of a Republican, Christian, Neo-Conservative majority who identified 'values' as being what motivated them to re-elect George W. Bush. In response to this, a Democrat strategy of preference accommodation would involve further concessions on issues such as abortion, gun control and gay rights that could fatally split its party coalition. The Democrats need to find a way of shaping the preferences of the electorate, to make them more sympathetic to liberal values.

We saw in Chapter 5 how anti-technocrats have identified the discourse of individual responsibilities to the community as the vehicle for a new mode of governance. However, there is a marked discrepancy in how the community discourse is deployed in relation to different social groups. Some are more vulnerable to being governed in the name of community than others, apparently depending on the power of the subject group to resist disciplinary state strategies. Those lacking the organisation and resources to resist micro-management in the name of the wider 'decent' community – such as the unemployed, single mothers and asylum seekers – are subject to direct interventions aimed at shaping their behaviour. This is evident in legislation that utilises the benefits system, as well as direct micro interventions (curfews, parenting orders, anti-social behaviour orders). This targeting is underpinned by an unrelenting 'no rights without responsibilities' discourse. However, those able to challenge and even redefine the dominant understandings of community, such as business and media interests, are more likely to be subject to mere appeals to 'do the right thing' in the name of 'fairness', or the even less prescriptive 'efficiency'. This is evidenced in New Labour's preference for the *self*-regulation of powerful interests, or the use of minimal codes that carry little obligation, as in the case of spiralling director pay.

The Third Way understanding of community, then, is as a vehicle for economic modernisation and the electoral targeting of a culturally conservative middle class. Community has become a key tool of governance across all areas of policy, and the extent to which groups are subject to its impositions appears to depend upon their ability to mobilise against it. Given this centrality of community to the Third Way project, its reconstruction is vital to any alternative.

Reconstructing community

Two main alternative conceptions of community are offered by the Third Way's critics.[23] The first, in the tradition of the radical democrats discussed in Chapter 7, envisages a role for progressive politics as the *facilitator* of political engagement between concrete communities. This approach sees antagonism as constitutive of social life, and seeks to harness this through a vibrant democratic politics. The radical democratic notion of communities stands in contrast to the more deliberative notion of a dialogic democracy favoured by Giddens.[24] On Giddens' account, the role of formal politics is also the facilitation of democratic engagement. But where radical democrats see such engagement as consisting in the inevitable *conflict* between social groups, Giddens' dialogic model presumes the existence of rational, implicitly universal solutions that can be arrived at consensually. Bewes identifies a similar approach in the work of leading communitarian thinker Amitai Etzioni, who, he suggests, 'postulates an objective point of equilibrium arrived at, in theory, by means of a friendly dialogue between conflicting positions'.[25] The imprint of this approach is visible in the Third Way's seeking of 'win–win' solutions, which downplay the possibility of irreconcilable, structurally embedded antagonisms of the sort that radical democrats prioritise.

A second alternative understanding of community echoes social democratic perspectives. It emphasises democratising the cultural sphere in order to foster the active, participatory citizen that a solidaristic community requires. This approach recognises the tendency of market logic to colonise other areas of social life, and argues for public spaces which operate according to non-market criteria, such as a defined notion of public interest.[26] This space would also represent the cultural milieu in which civic identities might be developed. The strategy here is to shore up the public sphere, defending it against the encroachment of the market. This is to be achieved by handing over decision-making in key areas to individuals who do not operate according to an instrumentalist, market logic. Sociologist Nicos Mouzelis identifies these individuals as 'those actually entitled to transmit [culture] to the new generations (teachers, parents, priests)'.[27] Mouzelis and others promoting this approach call for a 'balanced interdependence between the logic of profit and productivity in the economic sphere, and the logic of individual autonomy and self-realization in the cultural sphere'.[28] In this cultural sphere it is hoped that reflexive individuals can flourish, and dialogic democracy occur free from market imperatives. The effect would be to prevent the market economy from becoming a market society.

These alternative approaches to community resist the top-down, universalising version deployed by Third Wayers. However, if a more recognisably leftist version is to be developed, its substantive *content* needs addressing. Both of the above alternatives lack a critique of the market framework within which communities would continue to operate. This is where more traditional left criticism again has a role.

Radical democrats reject the Third Way's invocation of a single community, 'the people', and associated attempts to gloss over social antagonisms. Instead, they favour explicit recognition of the antagonism that, as we saw in Chapter 7, is held to be constitutive of social life. However, simply calling for the recognition of opposed social interests, and even their formal institutionalisation in the political sphere, does not provide a basis for a leftist reconstruction of community. In order to advance on both the model of dialogic democracy offered by Giddens, and the antagonistic approach of the radical democrats, the distortion of democratic exchange owing to the unequal distribution of power and resources needs to be addressed. Consequently, a reconstructed notion of community requires a critique of the inequalities generated by the social context in which politics is conducted. It needs to propose a *content* for the community it is advocating. It also needs to take an attitude towards the character of the antagonisms that it identifies. At present, the Third Way denies or glosses over structurally produced antagonisms, while radical democrats recognise them but ultimately seek simply their facilitation. In an advocacy of the radical democratic community, Little acknowledges the failure of radical democrats to develop a political economy that might address the sources of social and political marginalisation. But radical democrats are unlikely ever to undertake such a project, given their 'post-Marxist' *raison d'être*. Thus, Little concludes rather tamely that given 'exclusion and power can never be overcome', radical democrats can at least argue towards a framework in which 'the principles of democracy and value pluralism form the basis of more open and widespread democratic engagement'.[29] However laudable this desire for 'democratic engagement' is, it is difficult to distinguish from simple liberal pluralism. A more distinctively left reconstruction would go on to challenge the various structural *sources* of social and political inequality that underpin antagonisms and systematically generate exclusion. This harder-edged approach need not involve resorting back to Marxian economic reductionism; just the recognition that systemic inequalities exist and can be addressed through political intervention.

Similar points apply to the defensive social democratic model of community, outlined above, in which certain social spheres are protected from market imperatives. While this approach recognises the colonising nature of market logic, there is a tendency to reduce this process to the fact that:

> control of [today's] formidable cultural technologies is increasingly concentrated in the hands of a few economically powerful but democratically unaccountable individuals, whose policies follow more an economic/market logic and less a cultural-emancipatory logic.[30]

This analysis is voluntaristic in its implication that a change of *personnel* is sufficient to create new democratic spaces. There is the sense of a conspiracy theory amongst various elites, particularly those who control the media, who are depriving the wider population of the opportunity to develop their own identities in a dialogic democracy. This account also *underestimates* the tendency of the economic sphere to dominate all others. It was noted in Chapter 7 that an adequate analysis of the social conditions framing political strategies needs to understand the effects of macro social processes upon *all* actors – including elites. Simply arguing for the control of decision-making to be handed over to the 'right' individuals fails to account for the breadth and depth of market logic. Such an approach implies that there are some actors who embody market logic, and some who do not. It also suggests that individuals might somehow operate according to the logic of the market in the sphere of work, and then pursue their reflexive selves in the dialogic sphere of culture (presumably after work). But all social actors, whatever sphere of social life they are operating in, are strongly influenced by the burgeoning market logic that increasingly frames *all* action.

The limits to these alternative versions of community suggest where a distinctively left inflection might be given to the Third Way. To be sure, it is necessary to recognise structural antagonisms within the community, and to attempt to create spaces free from the encroachment of the market. But a more substantive view of the *content* of the desired community, and how it is to be achieved, needs to be adopted. Put bluntly, this necessitates giving greater weight to the more traditional left critique of how the operations of markets, and particularly the inequalities that they produce, obstruct the building of solidaristic communities.

There are obvious ways in which the Third Way could open up a more egalitarian agenda with regard to community. Attempts at encouraging behaviour in the interests of an imagined, universal community need to be directed more equally towards different social groups. At present, the Third Way targets weaker, marginal social actors in an effort to 'include' them in the community. But such efforts inevitably come up against the structural inequalities that *systematically* exclude and disadvantage such groups. Recognising this, the doctrine of 'no rights without responsibilities' could acknowledge that a minimum level of rights is required *before* all responsibilities can be adequately fulfilled.[31] This also applies to 'including' more powerful social groups who tend to *self-exclude* themselves.[32] Thus, in addition to pointing to the threat to social cohesion posed by excluded groups at the bottom, similar problems created by 'gated communities' and the withdrawal of the wealthy from large areas of public life could be highlighted. This might provide a discursive basis for arguments in favour of, for example, genuinely comprehensive education and health systems, on the grounds that private provision leads to social exclusion. Underpinning this, the case for more egalitarian policies can be made in terms of achieving the Third Way values of equal worth and equal opportunity. As Levitas notes in a restatement of the egalitarian case, 'if you accept the initial principle, endorsed on more than one occasion by Blair, that people are of equal worth, then a much stronger defence of substantive equality, or equality of condition, follows'.[33]

Building support for more egalitarian policies involves creating the normative climate to give such a strategy contemporary resonance. In contrast to the proceduralism of the radical democratic approach in particular, the *ends* of the desired community need to be argued for: it needs to be given a *content* that people want to buy into. It is at this point that the interrelation between the discourses of individualisation as autonomy, and community as empowerment, are clearest. In the same vein as Giddens' model of generative, bottom-up decision-making, the community can be envisaged as the site where solidaristic values are nurtured. To this end, the earlier New Labour discourse of using strong, cohesive communities as the vehicle for individual empowerment needs to be recovered. This could involve a move away from the celebration of the accrual of material wealth, and towards stressing the value of a greater range of contributions to the community. This includes valuing public sector workers of course, but also the voluntary work, caring, regeneration and similar activities that are undertaken by a range of individuals. Summarising the many critics of New Labour's model of 'productive' labour, Fitzpatrick notes that 'New Labour's espousal of the employment ethic narrows the accepted range of socially valuable activity and demoralises other forms of citizenship that do not orbit around wage earning, but which are equally valuable, if not more so.'[34] Promoting other types of valuable activities must not, of course, only take the form of a change in discursive strategy, but also recognise the increasingly important *economic* contribution that they make. To adapt Gordon Brown's slogan of 'fair is efficient' – we might say also that 'care is efficient' – and be prepared to further materially support activities that serve the wider community.

Just as with individualisation, then, community has taken on a conservative character in the Third Way. Radical democratic attempts at reworking community, as well as arguments for defending a public sphere, offer a starting point for reconstruction. But for this to be a project of the left, it needs to address the substantive issues of materially including all sections of the community and developing solidaristic values. Crucially, the strategy of seeking simply to facilitate communities, and letting them develop 'spontaneously', is insufficient for a left alternative. Taking a definite view as to the character of the desired community requires it to be *acted* upon; the progressive community needs to be brought into being through political action. In this respect, a left reconstruction would share with the current Third Way the attempt to use a particular, imagined version of community as a political device – although one with a very different character. Consequently, again in common with the Third Way, the discursive vehicle for the left to achieve its vision of solidaristic, empowering communities is *modernisation*.

Modernisation: from commodification to democratisation

Modernisation is *the* mediating concept between sociological claims about the nature of a changing world, and the potential for political interventions to shape such change. The centrality of modernisation to the Third Way is outlined below, along with its relationship to ideas about individualisation and community. Challenges to Third Way modernisation are examined in the form of democratisation strategies which open up spaces for alternative 'modernisations'. However, as with individualisation and community, if modernisation is to comprise part of a left project, it needs to be given a more substantive content. Theorists need to specify the desired normative and material *outcomes* of a modernising project.

Third Way modernisation: 'there is no alternative'

Discourses of modernisation have played an important role in political projects since long before the Third Way. Presenting a political strategy as modernising automatically implies that alternative or oppositional strategies are unmodern, anti-modern or even reactionary – none of which labels are likely to benefit a modern political party. For the political left in particular, modernisation has been an important vehicle for outlining how its narrative of an alternative social future is to be achieved. This was as true of the calls for industrial modernisation in the former USSR, as it was of the much-quoted 'white heat of technological revolution' invoked for old Labour by Harold Wilson.

In the Third Way, modernisation has assumed still greater importance to the wider political project. Newman suggests that aligning itself with 'a meta-narrative of modernisation [in terms of] political as well as social and economic progress was one of New Labour's major ideological achievements'.[35] Modernisation can be seen to have four key functions in the Third Way project. Firstly, it has a strategic political role by representing what Gilbert has described as a 'hard-centre'. This is aimed at 'the marginalisation both of the authoritarian populist right and the democratising left', thus reinforcing claims as to the obsolescence of left and right.[36] This strategic use of modernisation rhetoric has been debated among the cultural critics of the Third Way. Mouffe suggests that Third Wayers have simply made an *analytical error* in identifying the demise of the categories of left and right, given that these categories reflect an irreducible social antagonism.[37] By contrast, Gilbert argues that Mouffe has misread the political function of modernisation. He suggests that Third Wayers are not merely trying to describe, through a discourse of modernisation, the decline of left and right, but are in fact attempting to *define* it. The Third Way is an acute form of hegemonic politics, which simultaneously presents 'old labour' and (rhetorically at least) neoliberalism as failed modernisation strategies.[38] Bewes develops this point by claiming that it is precisely the attempt to obliterate the categories of left and right that guarantees the *survival* of ideological politics:

> ...'modernisation' is a pure signifier, having as little to do with modernity as Thatcher's 'freedom of choice' had to do with either freedom or choice. 'Modernisation' gestures towards the end of politics and, in so doing, confirms the continuity of ideological politics.[39]

A second role for modernisation in the Third Way is to signify the external imperative of rapid social change which all actors (individuals, political parties, nation-states) must adapt to. At this level, as with certain versions of globalisation, modernisation is reified as a generalised process occurring 'out there', apparently not caused by, or conducive to the interventions of, any political agency. The 'catch-all' character of modernisation makes it particularly useful as a rhetorical device to be invoked in the name of imposing change upon a whole host of areas of governance, especially the public services. Again, if actors oppose the imperative to modernise, they are presented as being reactionary. Paradoxically, it is precisely this reified notion of modernisation as an external imperative that facilitates its third major function in Third Way discourse: as the *process* which Third Way governments will undertake, or at least encourage others to undertake for themselves. Here modernisation again adopts an open-ended and 'catch-all' character. It becomes the justification for the centralisation of some powers, and the hiving off of others; it is a device for the granting or withdrawal of opportunities by the state.

Finally, modernisation provides a mechanism for linking discourses of individualisation and community. As Finlayson suggests:

> The party needs a 'team', a 'community' of some sort to be the body that both experiences and undertakes modernisation ... so that there is someone or something to appeal to in the name of modernisation ... The national/communal aspect of the modernisation project introduces the dimension of civil society ... It is a project of which everyone is a part and having everyone be part of it is one of the things that defines it.[40]

In Third Way discourse, then, the individual and community are simultaneously the objects and the tools of modernisation, as well as reinforcing each other. Individuals are the objects of modernisation when required to update their skills, practices and mindsets to meet the demands of the new economy. Simultaneously, it is those same individuals who are the tools for taking responsibility for this modernisation, as the state shifts from being direct provider to facilitator. The community is an object of modernisation, in the sense of national renewal. But community is also a vehicle: it is often in the name of national renewal that the strategy of individual modernisation is legitimised.

Critics of Third Way modernisation recognise that it is ripe for being given a different political inflection.[41] Many start by challenging the reification of modernisation as a process 'out there', and reclaim it as something over which actors have control and in which political content matters. Challenging the Third Way claim of German SPD leader, Gerhard Schroeder, that 'there were no politically distinct economic policies, only modern and unmodern ones', Birnbaum argues:

> Our reading of institutional change, however, is invariably conditioned by our political perspectives, our identification of agencies of change, our sense of the possibilities of transformation. The designation of a project as modern is not a judgement of fact, like the finding of a laboratory scientist, but an interpretation of our situation.[42]

The acceptance that modernisation will always be an active, strategic exercise rather than just a passive response to the external environment opens up a second key set of criticisms: that what goes under the guise of Third Way 'modernisation' is the deliberate extension of processes of *commodification*. What the apparently neutral language of a 'modernising process' masks are highly political decisions concerning the extension of the market into more areas of social life. The presentation of modernisation as a technocratic exercise, above ideological imperatives, is particularly important to New Labour. Unable to openly advocate the free market quite as aggressively as the Conservatives, New Labour have found in modernisation the vehicle for extending neoliberalism. At the same time, they are still able to distance themselves from their more explicitly neoliberal electoral competitors. As Bewes notes:

> The capitulation of the country, including the few remaining pockets of socialism, to the principles of market economics is a huge ideological project, *for which the concept of modernisation is a powerful, far from neutral, polemical baton.* [emphasis added][43]

A third criticism of Third Way modernisation is an interesting variant on this approach. Rather than Third Way neoliberalism being criticised, it is the *old left* character of modernisation that comes under fire, for being a vehicle for increasing centralisation. Thus, Desai bemoans the fact that 'The Third Way remains statist ... It perpetuates old left nostrums when the going gets tough.'[44] Similarly Marquand suggests that the New Labour state 'could scarcely be less aloof. It is a nagging, interfering presence in every corner of social life, imbued with a culture of command and control.'[45] On this view, the primary focus of Third Way modernisation is not necessarily increasing commodification (although this may feature strongly), but state micro-management of various services, most notably through extending regulation regimes of auditing and targets. Modernisation must be 'thoroughly monitored, audited and proven to exist'.[46]

Critics of Third Way modernisation are thus agreed that it represents a smokescreen, hiding either increasing commodification and/or centralisation of 'command and control' state power: this mirrors neo-Marxist and anti-technocratic criticisms. However, we shall see below that as in the case of both individualisation and community, the main alternative currently suggested – democratisation – lacks some of the most important insights of these criticisms. While democratisation is an important element *towards* a reconstructed modernisation, it does not on its own give the alternative a left character.

Democratisation and modernisation

The present Third Way has a very restricted understanding of democracy. Finlayson suggests that, as a result of the commodified view of individualism adopted by New Labour, there is a tendency to see democracy as merely facilitating an unmediated relationship between governing elites and the governed. This amounts to 'a form of consultation ... but not necessarily participation', based on an attachment to market principles even in the political sphere.[47] He argues for the recovery of a richer sense of democratic participation:

> Such 'marketisation' is antithetical to democratisation. Marketisation implies that it is enough for the individual simply to make a political purchase from the range of choices already available, and encourages a form of politics oriented towards preference accommodation rather than preference shaping. But true democratisation involves expanding the range of choices conceivable, making it possible to change the terms of choice and to alter the range of options available ... Democracy is not reducible to the aggregation of individual market choices. It is a transformative process that can alter ways of thinking about society and our place within it.[48]

Others go on to claim that a democratising project of modernisation might even have an *intrinsically* left character. Thus, Mouzelis sees the democratisation of the cultural sphere as the final stage in the development of various forms of rights. These rights correspond to different stages in the evolution of modernity: civil, political, social and now cultural. We have seen that Giddens describes struggles over cultural rights as representing a new form of 'life politics' (concerned with issues of identity and lifestyle), following the successful resolution of previous 'emancipatory' politics (concerned with power and inequality). However, Mouzelis sees the quest for cultural recognition as a *continuation* of the emancipatory struggle, in which the left/right divide remains as relevant as ever. Mouzelis seems to assume that democratising the cultural sphere will *necessarily* lead to its protection from the encroachment of the market.[49]

A strategy of understanding modernisation as democratisation certainly addresses each of the criticisms of the Third Way version outlined above. Firstly, it recognises the political, agentially driven character of any modernising project and seeks to bring it under democratic control: there is a space to negotiate the objectives of modernising processes. Secondly, with the ends of modernisation democratised, a debate can be held as to how far this should or should not involve increasing commodification. With the extent of commodification thus defined as a *political* decision, alternative criteria, such as a negotiated conception of the public interest in relation to markets, can come into play. Thirdly, successful democratisation will necessarily involve further devolution of responsibility for the design and delivery of modernising processes. This is in direct contrast to the centralising tendencies of the Third Way.

However, while democratisation must necessarily inform a reconstructed modernisation discourse, on its own it is an essentially procedural concept that can make no particular claim to be of the left. By itself, the call to democratisation is unlikely to attract or cultivate a left coalition. For example, Mouzelis attempts to map various types of rights onto different stages of modernity, culminating in the quest to secure cultural rights in the age of reflexivity. However, if claims for cultural rights are the logical corollary of reflexive modernity, it is not clear why it is necessarily the left who should be their main champion, nor the right who should oppose them. The specific areas that Mouzelis cites as reinforcing the left/right divide concern preservation of cultural and environmental integrity.[50] The first of these involves the freedom to forge one's own identity, and to have that identity recognised by others. However, much of the criticism of the old left is precisely its inability to appreciate the emerging diversity of lifestyles and their centrality to a changing political agenda. The 'New Times' critics contrasted this with the success of Thatcherism in elaborating narratives of freedom and choice that appealed to an (albeit restricted) sense of the opportunity to forge one's own biography.[51] Furthermore, the neoliberals' attack upon vested interests in the name of 'freedom' and 'opportunity' was easily discursively aligned with a commitment to democracy, despite the centralising tendencies of Thatcherism. There is an emphasis within traditional conservatism, too, on promoting the type of strong civic institutions that modern democratic theorists seek to cultivate (for example, Burke's much-quoted 'little platoons'). Thus, there is no *necessary* connection between the left and the defence of democratic spaces within which identities can be developed. The political right are just as capable of laying claim to the mantle of democracy – a fact being brutally confirmed by the ambitions of US neoconservatives to 'democratise' the globe.

Democratisation, then, is of itself insufficient to reconstruct a modernising strategy for the left – it lacks an explicitly leftist political *content*. This is inadvertently illustrated by those who – from a variety of perspectives – specifically highlight and endorse democratisation's *non-political* character. For such commentators, the problem of contemporary governance is how to manage an increasingly *complex* society. The burgeoning 'governance' literature is premised on the view that the top-down, command-and-control state cannot cope with governing dynamic, complex and fragmenting societies, and looks to new forms of democratic networks.[52] From a more critical perspective, Hirst presents his version of 'associational democracy' as his own third way between state socialism and *laissez-faire* economics. Yet even here, Hirst advocates associationalism, devolution and pluralism not on the basis of any intrinsic normative worth, but because such mechanisms are appropriate to managing social complexity. Hirst suggests that on this basis modernisation – understood as associational democracy – is of appeal to both the political left and right.[53] This depoliticising tendency is taken to its extreme in Geyer's attempt to locate Third Way theory as part of a paradigm shift towards complexity and open-endedness in the social sciences. On this basis, Geyer's criticism of Giddens' Third Way is that it is *not modernising enough*. For Geyer, the problem with Giddens' framework is the residual attempt to preserve the Third Way as a project of the left. Geyer argues that 'there is no reason for the Third Way to be an inherently leftist strategy. A complexity framework implies uncertainty for both left and right.'[54]

These accounts reflect the functional and historical confluence strands in Third Way thinking that were identified as problematic in Chapter 3. Mouzelis envisages modernisation as the evolution of different forms of rights which can be read off from a particular stage of modernity; this represents the most reductionist form of the functional approach to social change. Similarly, analysts of the new governance see a historical confluence between complexity and democratisation: democracy is reduced to a form of management.

Linking modernisation, individualisation and community

Repoliticising modernisation as a tool for the left requires an emphasis upon its *normative* character. What are the values that drive modernisation; what type of society do we want to modernise into being? These questions need to be addressed in a way that gives modernisation a distinctively left inflection, without slipping into the voluntarism that loses sight of structural conditions and was cautioned against in Chapter 3. By drawing on a reconstructed understanding of individualisation and community, modernisation *can* specify programmatic outcomes and offer a definite left vision. To achieve this, modernisation needs to be understood as a politically led, uneven and contested process. This would differentiate it from its reified, 'there is no alternative' form in the present Third Way. Significantly, this would also stand in contrast to the teleological models of social development that Giddens and others criticise for being adopted by the old left. Additionally, modernisation should indeed be equated with democratisation. However, in contrast to the critics discussed above, democratisation should be seen not as the objective or endpoint of modernisation, but rather as the *vehicle* for more substantive left objectives.

It has been shown throughout how the themes of individualisation, community and modernisation reinforce one another in the Third Way. These themes would remain interdependent within a left reconstruction. A left version of the politically led, democratised notion of modernisation would have as its objectives a developmental individualisation, understood as autonomy, enabled by a solidaristic version of community. Democratised modernisation *opens the way* for the left to argue that it is its own definition of individualisation and community that is modernisation's goal. In particular, this involves uncoupling our understanding of modernisation from com-modification, as they are currently conflated in the Third Way. Indeed, increasing commodification could come to viewed as regres-sive, an obstacle to modernisation thus conceived. In the nineteenth century, the old landed interests came to be seen as a hindrance to modernisation, understood as the establishment of free markets and liberal democracy. In the mid-twentieth century, the recognition of the limits of untrammelled markets led to modernisation strategies of increased social and economic planning. In the 1970s and 1980s, the tide turned again as neoliberals successfully portrayed the corporatist welfare state as the obstacle to modernisation, understood as the deregulation of finance capital. From the perspective of the left, the Third Way has been at best an inadequate attempt to reverse this neoliberal understanding of modernisation, and at worst its radical extension. The task for a post-Third Way left could be to achieve a common-sense understanding of modernisation as the building of a solidaristic community, aimed at creating the conditions for individ-ual development and autonomy. Vitally, this may involve extensive processes of *decommodification* – or 'rolling back' the market from areas of social life where its operations are inappropriate. In direct contrast to the rhetoric of the present Third Way, the left/right distinction – understood as modernisation projects conflicting over the role and extent of commodification – remains central.

Summary: after New Labour

The starting point of this book was that the Third Way – as an ongoing analysis of how the centre-left must engage with social transformation – has the potential for a more progressive reconstruc-tion. The Third Way has been most clearly elaborated by New Labour, but it is not reducible to their actions in government. Third Way thinking – whatever new labels it is given – has implications for the centre-left that stretch well beyond the New Labour project. A model was developed of how the Third Way implicitly understands the impact of sociological shifts upon the categories of left and right, as well as the nature of the relations between social change and political values (Part I). The Third Way has thus far failed to develop a narrative that shows how its values are grounded in contemporary social realities *and* can steer them towards inspiring, progressive goals. Preserving the left/right distinction is a prerequisite of such a strategy. The Third Way's various left critics have reproduced some of its own analytical limitations, but nevertheless provide the necessary critique of power and the effects of social commodification that can inform the defence of a left/right dichotomy (Part II). These strengths were combined with a cultural critique of the Third Way – recognising the importance of aligning political values with the grain of social transformation. The result was a framework for thinking through the development of centre-left strategies in an age of rapid social change. Drawing on this framework, this final chapter has sketched out three interrelated themes that illustrate how the Third Way might take a more progressive turn: individualisation, community and modernisation.

New Labour's Third Way has translated the sociological process of individualisation into an atomised 'utility maximisation', alongside cultural conservatism. But, in the knowledge economy, we can arrive at a more developmental sense of individualisation as autonomy. To achieve this we need a more critical attitude to the market instrumentalism which increasingly frames our sense of individuality. There is enormous scope for work and other activities to fall outside the restrictive, economically instrumental paradigm. Community is the site where a more autonomous, developmental individual could flourish. New Labour's sense of community is highly conservative; it is a vehicle for governing individuals for the purposes of neoliberal economic modernisation, and imposing culturally conservative norms which pander to the imagined demographic of Middle England. Critics of this Third Way community have proposed revitalising democracy through facilitating antagonism, and protecting and democratising the cultural sphere. But while democratisation is important for providing the spaces from which to challenge existing concentrations of power and resources, it does not advocate the substantive *transformation* that a left project seeks. A left reconstruction needs to advocate a *content* for the desired community. To this end, examples were offered of universalising the notion of inclusion to cover rich and poor, and normatively and materially valuing a broader range of contributions to the community.

Modernisation illustrates how the elements of a reconstructed Third Way, like the present version, would be mutually reinforcing. The Third Way uses modernisation as a device for marginalising opponents on left and right. It functions rhetorically as a general external imperative, to which both the individual and community must adapt, as well as a process which will be enacted by the state. Critics of Third Way modernisation see it as a smokescreen for extending commodification and centralisation. They again turn to democratisation as a means of 'opening up' modernisation – making its political character explicit and bringing it under democratic control. However, understanding modernisation as democratisation again lacks the substantive content required by a left project, and could as easily be claimed by the political right as the left. A more distinctively left strategy would value the potential of democratisation in opening up political spaces, but go on to specify programmatic *outcomes*; modernisation would have a definite objective. Drawing the key themes together, modernisation could be aimed at creating the conditions for the autonomous, developmental individual operating in the context of a solidaristic community. In the face of this new 'common sense', it would be New Labour's view of the atomised, commodified individual and the culturally conservative community which would be seen as hindering modernisation. In a reversal, New Labour's Third Way would appear as part of the forces of conservatism, and the project of modernisation aligned with genuinely progressive ends.

Notes

Introduction

1. Giddens offers a brief overview of such critics, for the purpose of dismissing them, in his *The Third Way and its Critics* (2000).
2. The most influential advocacy of stakeholding is Hutton's *The State We're In* (1995); for debate on the theme see Kelly *et al.* (eds) *Stakeholder Capitalism* (1997). For a dissection of the relationship between communitarian thinking and the Third Way, see Hale *et al.* (eds) *The Third Way and Beyond* (2004).
3. Blair 'Speech to the Congress of the Party of European Socialists' (1997), cited in Driver and Martell *New Labour* (1998), p. 7.
4. Hoggart 'No joke for No. 10 when a Hague gag hits the target' (1999).
5. Giddens *Where Now for New Labour?* (2002a), p. 3.
6. Blair 'Where the Third Way goes from here' (2003a).
7. Clinton 'A plan for the future' (2003).
8. Giddens 'Neoprogressivism' (2003).
9. Callinicos *Against the Third Way* (2001), p. 13. For further discussion of why its critics should take the Third Way seriously, see Leggett 'Criticism and the future of the Third Way' (2004a).
10. Etzioni *The Third Way to a Good Society* (2000); Collins 'Is there a Third Way in labour law?' (2001); Leadbetter 'Third Way on the beach' (2004).
11. The leader in this field is clearly Giddens; see his *The Third Way* (1998); *The Third Way and Its Critics* (2000); 'Neoprogressivism' (2003). For similarly theoretical, but critical accounts, see Callinicos *Against the Third Way* (2001); Touraine *Beyond Neoliberalism* (2001); Hale *et al.* (eds) *The Third Way and Beyond* (2004).
12. See e.g., Bewes and Gilbert (eds) *Cultural Capitalism* (2000); Driver and Martell *New Labour* (1998) and *Blair's Britain* (2002); Finlayson *Making Sense of New Labour* (2003); Pierson *Hard Choices* (2001).
13. See, for example, various contributions to Giddens (ed.) *The Global Third Way Debate* (2001); Tam (ed.) *Progressive Politics in the Global Age* (2001); White (ed.) *New Labour* (2001). Although not always explicitly focused on the Third Way, the concept frequently informs analyses of specific policy areas with regard to New Labour: see e.g., various contributions to Coates and Lawler (eds) *New Labour in Power* (2000); Lawson and Sherlock (eds) *The Progressive Century* (2001); Ludlam and Smith (eds) *New Labour in Government* (2001) and *Governing as New Labour* (2004); Seldon (ed.) *The Blair Effect* (2001).
14. For an account of the Third Way as a particular *mode* of idea, see McLennan 'Travelling with vehicular ideas' (2004).

15. The DLC's key documents are archived on its website, www.ndol.org.
16. Blair *The Third Way* (1998). Blair brought the Third Way to a wider audience by, for example, referring to it in his 1999 Leader's Speech.
17. Giddens' programmatic statement is his *Where Now for New Labour?* (2002a). He places his ideas in an updated political context in his 'Neoprogressivism' (2003).
18. Giddens 'Did they foul up my Third Way?' (2004), p. 25.

1   Third Way Sociology

1. Driver and Martell *New Labour* (1998), p. 27.
2. Finlayson's *Making Sense of New Labour* (2003) is a notable exception.
3. Cited in interview material with journalist Michael Cockerell; 'An inside view on Blair's Number 10' (2001), p. 574.
4. Wright *Why Vote Labour?* (1997a) p. 110.
5. Rustin 'The third sociological way' (2001), p. 13.
6. Giddens *Beyond Left and Right* (1994), ch. 3 and *The Third Way* (1998), ch. 2.
7. A number of the themes pursued by Giddens are mirrored in the work of Ulrich Beck. On the globalisation–individualisation relationship, see Beck *What is Globalization?* (2000). Giddens describes, 'The reflexivity of modernity' in his *The Consequences of Modernity* (1990), pp. 36–45. For debate over the social consequences of reflexivity see Beck *et al. Reflexive Modernization* (1994). Beck summarises the debate, in the context of his work on the implications for politics, in his *Democracy Without Enemies* (1998), chs. 7–8.
8. The most influential statement of the nature and effect of risk in contemporary societies remains Beck's *Risk Society* (1992).
9. Giddens *Beyond Left and Right* (1994), ch. 3. For an elaboration of the political consequences of this shift to a new form of modernity, see Beck *The Reinvention of Politics* (1997) and *Democracy Without Enemies* (1998).
10. Blair 'Leader's Speech' (1999).
11. Marquand 'Beyond left and right' (1989).
12. Giddens *The Third Way and Its Critics* (2000), p. 39.
13. Marquand 'Beyond left and right' (1989), p. 373.
14. Blair *The Third Way* (1998), p. 1.
15. Giddens *The Third Way* (1998); *The Third Way and its Critics* (2000); *Where Now for New Labour?* (2002a); 'Neoprogressivism' (2003).
16. Blair *The Third Way* (1998), p. 6.
17. Giddens *Beyond Left and Right* (1994), esp. chs. 1 and 2.
18. Ibid., ch. 4.
19. Brown 'Foreword' (1995), pp. 3–4.
20. Mulgan 'Uncertainty, reversibility and variety' (1989), p. 380.
21. Bellah and Sullivan 'Cultural resources for a progressive alternative' (2001), p. 21.
22. Wright *Who Dares Wins* (1997b), p. 5.
23. Driver and Martell 'Left, right and the third way' (2000), p. 154.

24. Blair 'Leader's Speech' (1999).
25. Giddens *The Third Way and Its Critics* (2000), p. 163.
26. Hay *The Political Economy of New Labour* (1999), p. 31.
27. For example, Hirst and Thompson *Globalization in Question* (1996).
28. For example, Dearlove 'Globalisation and the study of British politics' (2000).
29. For a concise overview of 'structural dependency' debates over globalisation see Wickham-Jones 'New Labour in the global economy' (2000).
30. Dearlove 'Globalisation and the study of British politics' (2000), p. 114.
31. Giddens *The Third Way and Its Critics* (2000), p. 73.
32. Ibid., p. 124. In the same volume, Giddens makes a point of emphasising the benefits of the market mechanism per se, p. 35.
33. Wickham-Jones 'New Labour in the global economy' (2000), p. 5.
34. Giddens *The Third Way and Its Critics* (2000), p. 52.
35. Ibid., p. 147.
36. See, for example, Amin (ed.) *Post-Fordism* (1994) and Hall and Jacques (eds) *New Times* (1989).
37. See, for example, Mulgan *Connexity* (1997); Terranova 'Of systems and networks' (2000).
38. Krieger *British Politics in the Global Age* (1999).
39. Giddens *The Third Way and Its Critics* (2000), p. 43.
40. An overview of the new political culture thesis, and the implications for left and right, is provided by Giddens, *The Third Way and Its Critics* (2000), pp. 40–4. Prior to this, Giddens also highlighted the increasing electoral significance of 'post-materialist' values; *The Third Way* (1998), pp. 19–23.
41. These concepts are elaborated in Giddens *Beyond Left and Right* (1994).
42. Giddens *The Third Way and Its Critics* (2000), p. 40.
43. See Driver and Martell 'New Labour: culture and economy' (1999).
44. Giddens *The Third Way and Its Critics* (2000), p. 38.
45. Heffernan 'Accounting for New Labour' (1996), p. 1286.
46. For a critical appraisal of the development of New Labour's discourse of 'social inclusion', see Levitas *The Inclusive Society?* (1998).
47. Annesley 'New Labour and welfare' (2001); Annesley and Gamble 'Economic and welfare policy' (2004).
48. Brown 'Foreword' (1995), p. 2.
49. Ibid., p. 3.
50. Giddens *The Third Way* (1998), ch. 4; Midgley 'Growth, redistribution and welfare' (1999).

2 Third Way Values

1. Jacques 'He risks leading his party into an electoral wilderness' (2004).
2. In addition to Blair and Giddens' respective *The Third Way* (1998), see, for example, Le Grand 'The Third Way begins with CORA' (1998); Latham 'The Third Way: an outline' (2001).
3. Giddens lists Third Way values as, 'Equality, protection of the vulnerable, freedom as autonomy, no rights without responsibilities, no authority

without democracy, cosmopolitan pluralism and philosophic conservatism.'
The Third Way (1998), p. 66.

4. Blair *The Third Way* (1998), p. 3.
5. The New Democrat statement derived from a 1990 meeting of the Democratic Leadership Council, the leading modernising Democrat group then chaired by Bill Clinton while a State Governor. The three core values identified were maintained and published in the new mission statement for New Democrats in 2000; Democratic Leadership Council 'The Hyde Park Declaration' (2000).
6. Blair 'Next steps for New Labour' (2002).
7. Blair *The Third Way* (1998), p. 3.
8. Ibid., p. 3.
9. Blair interviewed on *Today*, BBC Radio 4, 14 May 2001.
10. Blair 'Leader's Speech' (2004c) and 'Speech to the IPPR' (2004d).
11. Giddens *The Third Way* (1998), pp. 101–4.
12. See, for example, Selznick 'A quest for community' (2001).
13. For a critical appraisal of the relationship between the thinking of MacMurray and Blair, see Hale 'The communitarian "philosophy" of New Labour' (2004).
14. Blair *The Third Way* (1998), p. 4.
15. Crick 'Still missing: a public philosophy?' (1997), p. 346.
16. See, for example, Smith *New Questions for Socialism* (1996), p. 3.
17. Blair 'Leader's Speech' (2000).
18. Levitas *The Inclusive Society?* (1998), p. 110.
19. Crick 'Still missing: a public philosophy?' (1997), p. 347.
20. Ibid., p. 347.
21. Collins 'Community, morality and fairness' (1996), p. 32.
22. Giddens *The Third Way and Its Critics* (2000), p. 64.
23. For example, Dahrendorf 'Whatever happened to liberty?' (1999).
24. White 'The Third Way: not one road, but many' (1998), pp. 18–19.
25. Blair *The Third Way* (1998), p. 3.
26. Blair (2004a) Prime Minister's speech on Home Office and Criminal Justice System strategy.
27. Driver and Martell cite Blair's critique of old left and New Right on these grounds; *New Labour* (1998), p. 28.
28. Blair *The Third Way* (1998), p. 4. Blair had previously made, 'The rights we enjoy reflect the duties we owe' the title of his 1995 *Spectator* lecture.
29. Giddens *The Third Way* (1998), p. 65.
30. Le Grand makes 'accountability' the fourth key Third Way value, alongside community, opportunity and responsibility; 'The Third Way begins with CORA' (1998).
31. Giddens *Beyond Left and Right* (1994).
32. White identifies the key normative divisions among Third Wayers as 'leftists' vs centrists' with regard to opportunity, and 'liberals' vs 'communitarians' with regard to responsibilities and obligations, 'The ambiguities of the Third Way' (2001), pp. 11–13.

33. Crouch 'The Terms of the Neo-Liberal Consensus' (1997), p. 358.
34. Quoted in the *Financial Times*, 23 October 1998.
35. Allen 'Stakeholding by any other name' (2001), pp. 280–1.
36. Fairclough *New Labour, New Language?* (2000) p. 12.
37. Burnham 'New Labour and the politics of depoliticisation' (2001).
38. Hall and Jacques (eds) *The Politics of Thatcherism* (1983).
39. Levitas *The Inclusive Society?* (1998).
40. Gamble *The Free Economy and the Strong State* (1994).
41. Driver and Martell 'Left, right and the Third Way' (2000), pp. 159–60.
42. Freeden 'The ideology of New Labour' (1999).
43. This relationship is explored by, for example, White 'Rights and responsibilities' (1999a); Wright 'Liberal socialism' (2001).
44. Vincent 'New ideologies for old?' (1998), p. 50.
45. Ibid., p. 57.
46. For example, Larkin 'New Labour and old revisionism' (2000).
47. Rubinstein 'How new is New Labour?' (1997), p. 340.
48. Rubinstein 'A new look at New Labour' (2000), p. 162.
49. Meredith 'New Labour: "the road less travelled"?' (2003).
50. Bale 'The logic of no alternative?' (1999), p. 199.
51. The range of criticisms suggesting that the Third Way lacks any substantive content are pointed to in Giddens *The Third Way and Its Critics* (2000), ch. 1; Newman and de Zoysa *The Promise of the Third Way* (2001), ch. 6. See also Fairclough *New Labour, New Language?* (2000).
52. Quoted in 'Blair pledges opportunity society', *The Guardian*, www.guardian.co.uk, 11 October 2004.
53. Pierson *Hard Choices* (2001).
54. Bevir 'New Labour: a study in ideology' (2000).

3 Analysing Social Change and Political Strategy

1. Hall *The Hard Road to Renewal* (1988); Rustin 'The future of post-socialism' (1995). See also Marquand *Decline of the Public* (2004) for an account of the Thatcherites' *Kulturkampf*.
2. Blair and Schroeder 'Europe: The Third Way/Die Neue Mitte' (1999), p. 159.
3. Giddens *Beyond Left and Right* (1994).
4. Ibid. This point is explored by Finlayson *Making Sense of New Labour* (2003); Leggett 'Reflexive modernization and reconstructing the Third Way' (2002); McLennan 'Travelling with vehicular ideas' (2004).
5. Giddens *Beyond Left and Right* (1994).
6. Giddens *The Third Way* (1998), pp. 64–5.
7. Ibid., p. 65.
8. Ibid., p. 64.
9. Blair *The Third Way* (1998), p. 1.
10. Pierson *Hard Choices* (2001), p. 132.

11. Miliband 'Introduction' (1994), p. 6.
12. Brown 'The politics of potential' (1994a), p. 122.
13. Blair 'Speech to the National Policy Forum' (2004b).
14. Brown 'The politics of potential' (1994a), p. 116.
15. A position often taken by Gordon Brown, who explicitly made such a case in his Fabian Society Pamphlet, *Fair is Efficient* (1994b).
16. Kapstein 'The Third Way and the international order' (1999), p. 380.
17. Ibid., p. 381.
18. Blair 'Leader's Speech' (2000).
19. Brown 'Chancellor's Speech' (2004).
20. Giddens, *Beyond Left and Right* (1994). A similar point is made by Marquand *The Progressive Dilemma* (1991), p. 227.
21. Blair 'Leader's Speech' (2000).
22. Brown 'Chancellor's Speech' (2000).
23. Blair 'Leader's Speech' (2001).
24. Latham 'The Third Way: An outline' (2001), p. 27.
25. Brown 'Chancellor's Speech' (2004).
26. Toynbee 'Blair trashed the 60s for the sake of a Tory one-liner' (2004).
27. Freedland 'Tony Blair's survival is an affront to our constitution' (2004).
28. Hay *The Political Economy of New Labour* (1999), p. 37. See also Benton 'Beyond left and right?' (1997).
29. Hay *The Political Economy of New Labour* (1999), p. 168.
30. Giddens 'Just carry on being new' (2001c), p. 30.
31. Giddens 'Neoprogressivism' (2003), p. 6.
32. Driver and Martell 'Left, right and the Third Way' (2000), p. 152.
33. Brown 'Chancellor's Speech' (2004).
34. Blair *The Third Way* (1998).

4 Neo-Marxists: *Capitalism with an (In)human Face*

1. Callinicos *Against the Third Way* (2001), p. 17.
2. Hirst and Thompson *Globalisation in Question* (1996).
3. Bromley 'Globalization?' (1996), p. 4.
4. For a critique of the 'new' sociology (concerning, for example, globalisa- tion, post-Fordism) and defence of the 'older' tools for analysing social policy, such as through class inequality and the nation-state, see, for example, Taylor-Gooby 'In defence of second-best theory' (1997).
5. Froud *et al.* 'The Third Way and the jammed economy' (1999), p. 157.
6. Callinicos *Against the Third Way* (2001), p. 67.
7. Benton 'Radical politics – neither left nor right?' (1999), p. 47. On the importance of the *idea* of globalisation amongst policy elites in actu- ally bringing it into being, see Hay *The Political Economy of New Labour* (1999).
8. Bourdieu and Wacquant 'NewLiberalSpeak' (2001), p. 4.

9. For a debate on the extent to which the knowledge economy represents a qualitative shift, or remains traditionally capitalist, see Giddens and Hutton 'In conversation' (2000).

10. The extent and implications of deepening domestic and global inequalities, under conditions of neoliberal globalisation, are outlined by Faux and Mishel 'Inequality and the global economy' (2001).

11. Froud *et al.* 'The Third Way and the jammed economy' (1999), p. 160. For an account of how accumulation imperatives, rather than new knowledge or technologies, drive organisational restructuring, see Clarke 'The crisis of Fordism or the crisis of social democracy?' (1990).

12. Giddens *The Third Way and Its Critics* (2000), p. 44.

13. Callinicos *Against the Third Way* (2001), p. 114.

14. Coates and Barratt Brown 'The Third Way to the servile state' (1999), pp. 41–2.

15. Jordan 'Globalization, exclusion and progressive economic policies' (2001).

16. See Callinicos (citing Bourdieu) 'Social theory put to the test of politics' (1999), p. 89.

17. McLennan 'Travelling with vehicular ideas' (2004), p. 492.

18. Callinicos *Against the Third Way* (2001), p. 124.

19. The global character of the capitalist class is outlined by Sklair in his *The Transnational Capitalist Class* (2001).

20. Crouch 'The terms of the neoliberal consensus' (1997), p. 354.

21. Crouch 'The parabola of working class politics' (1999), pp. 74–6. For an account of how maximising shareholder value has become the dominant conception of the firm, see Hutton *The State to Come* (1997).

22. Gilbert 'Beyond the hegemony of New Labour' (2000b), p. 229.

23. Webb and Fisher 'Professionalism and the Millbank Tendency' (2003), pp. 18–19.

24. Crouch *Post-Democracy* (2004), p. 72.

25. Bourdieu and Wacquant 'NewLiberalSpeak' (2001).

26. Gilbert 'Beyond the hegemony of New Labour' (2000b), p. 235.

27. Froud *et al.* 'The Third Way and the jammed economy' (1999), p. 162.

28. Ibid., p. 165.

29. Benton 'Clause 4' (1995), p. 4.

30. Hobsbawm 'The death of neo-liberalism' (1998), p. 8.

31. Callinicos *Against the Third Way* (2001), p. 116.

32. Ibid., p. 120.

33. See, for example, Cammack 'Giddens' way with words' (2004); Fairclough *New Labour, New Language?* (2000).

34. Callinicos 'Social theory put to the test of politics' (1999), p. 102.

35. Cammack 'Giddens' way with words' (2004), p. 165.

36. Callinicos *Against the Third Way* (2001), p. 121. The same point is made by Anderson 'Renewals' (2000).

37. Callinicos 'Social theory put to the test of politics' (1999), p. 84.

38. Lester 'Common sense, reality and the Third Way' (2000), p. 4.

39. Lester 'Common sense, reality and the Third Way' (2000), p. 4.
40. See, for example, Callinicos' analysis of Bourdieu's account of the 'traditional' social forces that might be marshalled to defend 'civilisation against the market'; 'Social theory put to the test of politics' (1999), pp. 90–2.
41. Callinicos *Against the Third Way* (2001), p. 59.
42. Watkins 'A weightless hegemony' (2004), pp. 32–3.
43. For an account of the Third Way as the latest instalment of a historically compromised social democratic reformism, see Przeworski 'How many ways can be third?' (2001).
44. For example, Callinicos 'Social theory put to the test of politics' (1999); Cammack 'Giddens' way with words' (2004); Miliband *Socialism for a Sceptical Age* (1994).
45. Watkins 'A weightless hegemony' (2004), p. 32.

5   Anti-Technocrats: *The Tyranny of Targets*

1. The classic statement of the 'technicisation' of politics from among the Frankfurt School writers is Marcuse's *One-Dimensional Man* (1964).
2. This encroachment is most famously captured by Habermas' account of the colonisation of the 'lifeworld' (where dialogue and politics is possible) by the 'system' (driven by the logic of money and bureaucracy); Habermas *The Theory of Communicative Action, Lifeworld and System* (1989).
3. Marcuse *One-Dimensional Man* (1964).
4. Rose *Powers of Freedom* (1999a), p. 235.
5. See, for example, Burch and Holliday 'New Labour and the machinery of government' (2000).
6. Terranova 'Of systems and networks' (2000), p. 124.
7. Frankel 'Confronting neoliberal regimes' (1997), p. 63.
8. Terranova 'Of systems and networks' (2000), p. 124.
9. Marcuse *One-Dimensional Man* (1964).
10. Kircheimer 'The transformation of the Western European party systems' (1966).
11. Finlayson 'Elements of the Blairite image of leadership' (2002).
12. For an account of the protracted struggle over control of Labour Party structures see Shaw *The Labour Party Since 1979* (1994) and, with reference to Blair's New Labour, Seyd and Whitely 'New Labour and the Party' (2001).
13. For a detailed account of New Labour's electoral strategy by their chief pollster, see Gould, *The Unfinished Revolution* (1999).
14. Mair 'Partyless democracy' (2000), p. 22.
15. Interviewed on BBC2 'Eight people sipping wine in Kettering' (2002).
16. Mair 'Partyless democracy' (2000), pp. 27–8.
17. Burnham 'New Labour and the politics of depoliticisation' (2001), p. 127.
18. Ibid., p. 129.
19. Rose and Miller 'Political power beyond the state' (1992), p. 174.
20. Ibid., p. 175.

21. Rose *Powers of Freedom* (1999a); 'Inventiveness in Politics' (1999b); 'Community, citizenship and the Third Way' (2001).
22. Rose 'Community, citizenship and the Third Way' (2001), p. 4. The Foucauldian approach is elaborated in relation to New Labour by Finlayson *Making Sense of New Labour* (2003), ch. 5.
23. Rose 'Community, citizenship and the Third Way' (2001), p. 5.
24. Rose *Powers of Freedom* (1999a), p. 176.
25. See, for example, Morrison 'New Labour, citizenship and the discourse of the Third Way' (2004).
26. Rose *Powers of Freedom* (1999a), p. 190.
27. Finlayson 'New Labour: the culture of government and the government of culture' (2000), p. 189.
28. Finlayson *Making Sense of New Labour* (2003), p. 155.
29. Rustin 'The third sociological way' (2001), p. 20.
30. Rose 'Community, citizenship and the Third Way' (2001), p. 12.
31. Marcuse *One-Dimensional Man* (1964).
32. Mair 'Partyless democracy' (2000), pp. 32–3.
33. Frankel 'Confronting neoliberal regimes' (1995), pp. 63–4.
34. For example, Allender 'What's new about "New Labour"?' (2001).

6 Social Democrats: *The Real Third Way?*

1. Giddens 'Introduction' (2001a), p. 2.
2. Giddens *Where Now for New Labour?* (2002a), p. 78.
3. Giddens 'Neoprogressivism' (2003), p. 2.
4. Blair 'Where the Third Way goes from here' (2003a).
5. Hay *The Political Economy of New Labour* (1999), pp. 56–7.
6. Merkel 'The Third Ways of social democracy' (2001), p. 51.
7. Giddens *The Third Way* (1998), p. 7.
8. Hay *The Political Economy of New Labour* (1999), pp. 56–7.
9. Pierson *Hard Choices* (2001), p. 56.
10. Giddens *The Third Way* (1998), p. 7; Pierson *Hard Choices* (2001), pp. 38–47.
11. Esping-Andersen *Politics Against Markets* (1985); Krieger *British Politics in the Global Age* (1999), ch. 3.
12. Gamble and Wright 'Introduction' (1999), p. 4.
13. Ibid., p. 6.
14. Gamble and Wright 'From Thatcher to Blair' (2001), p. 4.
15. *The Observer*, editorial, 21 April 2002.
16. Lawson *et al.* '(Not) as good as it gets' (2004).
17. Rawnsley 'New Labour grows up' (2002).
18. See www.policy-network.net.
19. Crouch *Post-Democracy* (2004); Fitzpatrick *After the New Social Democracy* (2003); Marquand *Decline of the Public* (2004).
20. Thompson and Gould 'Thompson vs. Gould' (2003), p. 5.
21. Lawson *et al.* '(Not) as good as it gets' (2004), p. 9.

22. Such an argument is made by Gray *After Social Democracy* (1996), and challenged by Pierson *Hard Choices* (2001).
23. For example, Garrett *Partisan Politics in the Global Economy* (1998).
24. Pierson *Hard Choices* (2001), p. 40.
25. Ibid., p. 45.
26. Marquand 'Premature obsequies' (1999), p. 10.
27. Pierson *Hard Choices* (2001) ch. 1.
28. Ibid., pp. 122 and 123.
29. Ibid., p. 109.
30. Hirst 'Globalisation and social democracy' (1999a).
31. Garrett *Partisan Politics in the Global Economy* (1998); Vandenbroucke 'European social democracy and the Third Way' (2001).
32. Pierson *Hard Choices* (2001), pp. 81–2.
33. For an overview of the debate, see Coates 'Capitalist models and social democracy' (2001).
34. Vandenbroucke *Globalisation, Inequality and Social Democracy* (1998), p. 50.
35. Ibid., p. 50.
36. Crouch *Post-Democracy* (2004).
37. Marquand 'Premature obsequies' (1999); *Decline of the Public* (2004).
38. Hutton *The State We're In* (1995); *The State to Come* (1997).
39. See, for example, Faux and Mishel 'Inequality and the global economy' (2000); Crouch *Post-Democracy* (2004).
40. Heath *et al. The Rise of New Labour* (2001).
41. Gamble and Wright 'From Thatcher to Blair' (2001), pp. 1–2.
42. Krieger *British Politics in the Global Age* (1999).
43. White 'Social liberalism, stakeholder socialism and post-industrial social democracy' (1999b), p. 36.
44. Interview on *Newsnight*, BBC2, 4 June 2001.
45. IPPR *State of the Nation* (2004); Commission on Social Justice *Social Justice* (1994).
46. Marquand *Decline of the Public* (2004), p. 45.
47. *New Statesman*, editorial, 22 April 2002, p. 4.
48. Hirst 'Globalisation and social democracy' (1999a), p. 89.
49. Giddens *Beyond Left and Right* (1994).
50. Blair 'Where the Third Way goes from here' (2003a), p. 4.
51. See, for example, the modernising polemic by Hombach *The Politics of the New Centre* (2000) and a defence from the traditional left by Lafontaine *The Heart Beats on the Left* (2000).
52. For example, Giddens 'The third way can beat the far right' (2002b).
53. Eagle 'A deeper democracy' (2003), p. 19.
54. See, for example, Hutton *The State We're In* (1995); *The State to Come* (1997), as well as his weekly column in *The Observer*.
55. For example, White 'Social liberalism, stakeholder socialism and post-industrial social democracy' (1999b); Wilson 'Liberal socialism and the future of progressive politics' (1999).
56. Jacobs 'Environmental democracy' (1999).
57. Blair 'Opening speech to the Progressive Governance Conference' (2003c).

58. See, for example, Held 'Global social democracy' (2003) and *Global Covenant* (2004). Giddens endorses the global social democratic approach in his 'Neoprogressivism' (2003).
59. Marquand *Decline of the Public* (2004) pp. 142–3.
60. Crouch, *Post-Democracy* (2004), p. 120.
61. Fitzpatrick *After the New Social Democracy* (2003), p. 206.

7 Developing the Critics

1. Heffernan *New Labour and Thatcherism* (2000), esp. ch. 2.
2. Such arguments are summarised by Finlayson *Making Sense of New Labour* (2003), ch. 6.
3. Miliband *Socialism for a Sceptical Age* (1994).
4. Callinicos *Against the Third Way* (2001).
5. Fitzpatrick *After the New Social Democracy* (2003), p. 26.
6. Anderson 'Comment: power, politics and the Enlightenment' (1994), p. 43. For examples of campaign strategising see Gould *The Unfinished Revolution* (1999) for a UK illustration, and Morris *Behind the Oval Office* (1997), for the US.
7. Callinicos *Against the Third Way* (2001), p. 35.
8. For a discussion of the nuances of historical left/right development in relation to previous 'third ways', see Bastow and Martin *Third Way Discourse* (2003), esp. pp. 22–39.
9. Bobbio *Left and Right* (1996 [1994]).
10. Salvati 'Prolegomena to the Third Way debate' (2001).
11. Clinton 'A plan for the future' (2003), p. 3.
12. This is a further theme of Roy Hattersley's critique of New Labour in his regular *Guardian* column. Giddens himself has also explicitly challenged the desirability of meritocracy as a Third Way goal; *The Third Way* (1998), pp. 101–4.
13. Crouch 'The parabola of working class politics' (1999); *Post-Democracy* (2004).
14. Mouzelis 'Reflexive modernization and the third way' (2001). See Leggett 'Reflexive modernization and reconstructing the Third Way' (2002) for a critique of the Mouzelis/Giddens encounter.
15. Lawson *et al.* '(Not) As good as it gets' (2004), p. 8.
16. Marquand *Decline of the Public* (2004).
17. Fitzpatrick develops an interesting argument, using similar tools, in his *After the New Social Democracy* (2003).
18. The original 'New Times' contributions are collected in Hall and Jacques (eds) *New Times* (1989). For further discussion of the development of the New Times analysis in relation to the Third Way, see Finlayson *Making Sense of New Labour* (2003), ch. 4. For an earlier overview of the development of New Times, see Davey 'Waking up to New Times' (1994).
19. Hall and Jacques (eds) *The Politics of Thatcherism* (1983).
20. Marquand *Decline of the Public* (2004), p. 89.
21. Ibid., p. 104.

22. Hall 'The great moving nowhere show' (1998), p. 14. See also Hall 'New Labour's double-shuffle' (2003).
23. Hall 'Interview: culture and power' (1997), pp. 30–1.
24. Finlayson *Making Sense of New Labour* (2003), p. 118.
25. Hall 'Interview: culture and power' (1997), p. 36.
26. Showstack Sassoon 'Gramsci and us' (1998), p. 161.
27. Finlayson *Making Sense of New Labour* (2003), p. 124. *Demos* is a London-based think-tank associated with New Labour. For a discussion of the tendency of political third ways to involve 'vanguardism', see Bastow and Martin *Third Way Discourse* (2003).
28. Gilbert 'Beyond the hegemony of New Labour' (2000b), p. 223.
29. For an account of the entrenchment of Thatcherite discourse, inspired by Hall's analysis, see Phillips 'Hegemony and political discourse' (1998). Hall's account of the hegemonic status of Thatcherism has been strongly challenged by political scientists on empirical grounds; see, for example, Crewe 'Has the electorate become Thatcherite?' (1988).
30. Marquand *Decline of the Public* (2004), p. 118.
31. Philo 'Politics, media and public belief' (1994), pp. 52 and 47.
32. For a theoretical statement of post-Marxism, see Laclau and Mouffe 'Post-Marxism without apologies' (1990) and Geras' 'Post-Marxism?' (1987) for an orthodox Marxist response.
33. For an elaboration of 'radical democracy', see Mouffe *Dimensions of Radical Democracy* (1992). Mouffe engages with the Third Way in her *The Democratic Paradox* (2000). Bastow and Martin present radical democracy as a progressive alternative to the Third Way in their *Third Way Discourse* (2003).
34. Wenman 'What is politics?' (2003), p. 60.
35. Finlayson *Making Sense of New Labour* (2003), p. 96.
36. Wenman 'What is politics?' (2003), p. 62.
37. Lent 'Radical democracy' (1994), p. 229. Little also argues for the redistributive credentials of radical democracy *contra* the Third Way; 'Community and radical democracy' (2002).
38. Mouffe '10 years of false starts' (1999), p. 20.
39. Wood 'Stuart Hall's cultural studies and the problem of hegemony' (1998), p. 409.
40. Ibid., p. 405.

8   Reconstructing the Third Way

1. Gilbert 'The second wave' (2004), p. 33.
2. For example, Finlayson *Making Sense of New Labour* (2003); Gilbert 'The second wave' (2004); Needham 'Customer-focused government' (2004).
3. Blair addressed these themes in speeches reported in the *Guardian*, 4 December 2004 and 14 January 2005.
4. Giddens *Beyond Left and Right* (1994).
5. Ibid. For further discussion of the progressive potential of Giddens' model, see Leggett 'Criticism and the future of the Third Way' (2004a)

and McCullen and Harris 'Generative equality, work and the Third Way' (2004).

6. For an argument from an 'old Labour' politician that individual freedom is the objective of socialism, see Hattersley *Choose Freedom* (1987).
7. Driver and Martell 'Left, right and the third way' (2000), p. 157; *Blair's Britain* (2002).
8. Rustin 'The future of post-socialism' (1995), p. 24. See also Bentley 'The Self-creating society' (2004).
9. Beck envisages future social and economic policy being framed by the emerging individualisation; *What is Globalization?* (2000).
10. For example, Mulgan and Briscoe 'The society of networks' (1997).
11. For example, Bentley 'Letting go' (2002); Geyer 'Beyond the Third Way' (2003).
12. For a discussion of the ideological intent behind such encroachment, see Shaw 'What matters is what works' (2004); Marquand *Decline of the Public* (2004).
13. Levitas *The Inclusive Society?* (1998), pp. 126–7.
14. Finlayson *Making Sense of New Labour* (2003), p. 166. See also Gilbert 'The second wave' (2004).
15. Hall 'The great moving nowhere show' (1998).
16. Gould *The Unfinished Revolution* (1999), p. 173, citing Greenberg 'Reconstructing the Democratic vision' (1990).
17. Ibid., pp. 85 and 172–5.
18. Ibid., p. 85.
19. Milburn 'Labour's contract for a third term' (2005).
20. Finlayson *Making Sense of New Labour* (2003).
21. Hay *The Political Economy of New Labour* (1999).
22. Bentley 'The Self-creating society' (2004), p. 5.
23. For further discussion of different political permutations of community, see Driver and Martell *Blair's Britain* (2002).
24. Giddens *Beyond Left and Right* (1994).
25. Bewes *Cynicism and Postmodernity* (1997), p. 86.
26. The autonomous logic of the public sphere is outlined by Marquand *Decline of the Public* (2004).
27. Mouzelis 'Reflexive modernization and the third way' (2001), p. 448.
28. Ibid., p. 449.
29. Little 'Community and radical democracy' (2002), p. 379.
30. Mouzelis 'Reflexive modernization and the third way' (2001), p. 448.
31. Lister 'Towards an inclusive society' (2001).
32. Giddens *The Third Way* (1998), pp. 101–4.
33. Levitas 'Shuffling back to equality?' (2004), p. 69. See also Westergaard 'Where does the third way lead?' (1999).
34. Fitzpatrick *After the New Social Democracy* (2003), pp. 48–9.
35. Newman *Modernising Governance* (2001), p. 54.
36. Gilbert 'Beyond the hegemony of New Labour' (2000b), p. 226.
37. Mouffe '10 Years of false starts' (1999).
38. Gilbert 'In defence of discourse analysis' (2000a).

39. Bewes 'Who cares who wins?' (1998), p. 207.
40. Finlayson *Making Sense of New Labour* (2003), p. 96.
41. For example, the search for alternative discourses of modernisation is a unifying theme of Bewes and Gilbert's critical edited collection on New Labour, *Cultural Capitalism* (2000).
42. Birnbaum 'Is the Third Way authentic?' (1999), p. 437.
43. Bewes 'Who cares who wins?' (1998), p. 194.
44. Desai 'Still waiting' (2000), p. 12.
45. Marquand *Decline of the Public* (2004), p. 125.
46. Finlayson *Making Sense of New Labour* (2003), p. 93.
47. Ibid., p. 133.
48. Ibid., p. 134.
49. Mouzelis 'Reflexive modernization and the third way' (2001). See also Leggett 'Reflexive modernization and reconstructing the Third Way' (2002).
50. Mouzelis, 'Reflexive Modernization', pp. 446–7.
51. See for example, Hall *The Hard Road to Renewal* (1988); 'The great moving nowhere show' (1998).
52. See Newman *Modernising Governance* (2001) for an outline and critical appraisal of the governance literature.
53. Hirst *From Statism to Pluralism* (1997). See also Hirst and Bader (eds) *Associative Democracy* (2001).
54. Geyer 'Beyond the Third Way' (2003), p. 254.

Bibliography

Allen, M. (2001) 'Stakeholding by any other name: a Third Way business strategy', in Giddens (ed.), *The Global Third Way Debate*.

Allender, P. (2001) 'What's new about "New Labour"?', *Politics*, 21:1 (February): 56–62.

Amin, A. (ed.) (1994) *Post-Fordism: a Reader*, Oxford: Blackwell.

Anderson, P. (1994) 'Comment: power, politics and the Enlightenment', in Miliband (ed.) *Reinventing the Left*.

Anderson, P. (2000) 'Renewals', *New Left Review*, 1:2 (January/February).

Annesley, C. (2001) 'New Labour and welfare', in Ludlam and Smith (eds), *New Labour in Government*.

Annesley, C. and Gamble, A. (2004) 'Economic and welfare policy' in Ludlam and Smith (eds), *Governing as New Labour*.

Arestis, P. and Sawyer, M. (eds) (2001) *The Economics of the Third Way*, Cheltenham: Edward Elgar.

Bale, T. (1999) 'The logic of no alternative? Political scientists, historians and the politics of Labour's past', *British Journal of Politics and International Relations*, 1:2 (June): 192–204.

Barrientos, A. and Powell, M. (2004) 'The route map of the Third Way', in Hale, Leggett and Martell (eds), *The Third Way and Beyond*.

Bastow, S. and Martin, J. (2003) *Third Way Discourse: European Ideologies in the Twentieth Century*, Edinburgh: Edinburgh University Press.

BBC2 (2002) 'Eight people sipping wine in Kettering', *Century of the Self* (episode 4), broadcast on 7 April.

Beck, U. (1992 [1986]) *Risk Society: Towards a New Modernity*, London: Sage.

Beck, U. (1997) *The Reinvention of Politics: Re-thinking Modernity in the Global Social Order*, Cambridge: Polity.

Beck, U. (1998) *Democracy Without Enemies*, Cambridge: Polity.

Beck, U. (2000) *What is Globalization?*, Cambridge: Polity.

Beck, U., Giddens, A. and Lash, S. (1994) *Reflexive Modernization: Politics, Tradition and Aesthetics in the Modern Social Order*, Cambridge: Polity.

Bellah, R.N. and Sullivan, W. (2001) 'Cultural resources for a progressive alternative', in Tam (ed.), *Progressive Politics in the Global Age*.

Bentley, T. (2002) 'Letting Go: complexity, individualism and the left', *Renewal*, 10:1. Accessed via www.policy-network.net, 24 May 2002.

Bentley, T. (2004) 'The Self-creating society', *Renewal*, 12:1. Accessed via www.renewal.org.uk.

Benton, T. (1995) 'Clause 4', *Radical Philosophy*, 72 (July/August): 2–4.

Benton, T. (1997) 'Beyond Left and Right? Ecological politics, capitalism and modernity', in Jacobs *et al.* (eds) *Greening the Millennium?*, Oxford: Blackwell.

Benton, T. (1999) 'Radical politics – neither Left nor Right?', in O'Brien *et al.* (eds), *Theorising Modernity.*

Bevir, M. (2000) 'New Labour: a study in ideology', *British Journal of Politics and International Relations,* 2:3 (October): 277–301.

Bewes, T. (1997) *Cynicism and Postmodernity,* London: Verso.

Bewes, T. (1998) 'Who cares who wins? Postmodernisation and the radicalism of indifference', in Coddington and Perryman (eds), *The Moderniser's Dilemma.*

Bewes, T. and Gilbert, J. (eds) (2000) *Cultural Capitalism: Politics after New Labour,* London: Lawrence & Wishart.

Birnbaum, N. (1999) 'Is the Third Way authentic?', *New Political Economy,* 4:3: 437–46.

Blair, T. (1995) 'The rights we enjoy reflect the duties we owe', *The Spectator* Lecture, London, 22 March.

Blair, T. (1997) Speech to the Congress of the Party of European Socialists, Malmo, 6 June.

Blair, T. (1998) *The Third Way: New Politics for the New Century,* Fabian Society Pamphlet 588, London: College Hill.

Blair, T. (1999) Leader's Speech to the Labour Party Conference, Bournemouth, 28 September.

Blair, T. (2000) Leader's Speech to the Labour Party Conference, Brighton, 26 September.

Blair, T. (2001) Leader's Speech to the Labour Party Conference, Brighton, 2 October.

Blair, T. (2002) 'Next steps for New Labour', speech delivered at the London School of Economics, London, 12 March.

Blair, T. (2003a) 'Where the Third Way goes from here', *Progressive Politics* (Policy Network), 2:1. Accessed via www.policy-network.net, 7 September 2004.

Blair, T. (2003b) 'Renewing progressive politics', *Progressive Politics* (Policy Network) 2:2. Accessed via www.policy-network.net, 7 September 2004.

Blair, T. (2003c) 'Opening speech to the *Progressive Governance Conference,* London, July 2003', in *Progressive Politics* (Policy Network), 2:3. Accessed via www.policy-network.net, 7 September 2004.

Blair, T. (2004a) Prime Minister's speech at the launch of the Home Office and Criminal Justice System strategic plan, 19 July.

Blair, T. (2004b) Speech to the Labour Party National Policy Forum, University of Warwick, 24 July.

Blair, T. (2004c) Leader's Speech to the Labour Party Conference, Brighton, 28 September.

Blair, T. (2004d) Speech to the IPPR, 11 October.

Blair, T. and Schroeder, G. (1999), 'Europe: The Third Way/Die Neue Mitte', in Hombach, *The Politics of the New Centre.*

Bobbio, N. (1996) (1994) *Left and Right: the Significance of a Political Distinction,* Cambridge: Polity.

Bourdieu, P. and Wacquant, L. (2001) 'NewLiberalSpeak: notes on the planetary vulgate', *Radical Philosophy,* 105 (January/February): 2–5.

Bromley, S. (1996) 'Globalization?', *Radical Philosophy,* 80 (November/December): 2–5.

Brown, G. (1994a) 'The politics of potential: a new agenda for Labour', in Miliband (ed.), *Reinventing the Left*.

Brown, G. (1994b) *Fair is Efficient: a Socialist Agenda for Fairness*, Fabian Pamphlet 563, London: College Hill.

Brown, G. (1995) 'Foreword', in Crouch and Marquand (eds), *Re-inventing Collective Action*.

Brown, G. (2000) Chancellor of the Exchequer's Speech to the Labour Party Conference, Brighton, September.

Brown, G. (2004) Chancellor of the Exchequer's Speech to the Labour Party Conference, September.

Burch, M. and Holliday, I. (2000) 'New Labour and the machinery of government', in Coates and Lawler (eds), *New Labour in Power*.

Burnham, P. (2001) 'New Labour and the politics of depoliticisation', *British Journal of Politics and International Relations*, 3:2 (June): 127–49.

Callinicos, A. (1999) 'Social theory put to the test of politics: Pierre Bourdieu and Anthony Giddens', *New Left Review*, 236 (I) (July/August): 77–102.

Callinicos, A. (2001) *Against the Third Way: An Anti-Capitalist Critique*, Cambridge: Polity.

Cammack, P. (2004) 'Giddens' way with words', in Hale, Leggett and Martell (eds), *The Third Way and Beyond*.

Clarke, S. (1990) 'The crisis of Fordism or the crisis of social democracy?', *Telos*, 83 (Spring): 71–98.

Clinton, B. (2003) 'A plan for the future', speech to the *Progressive Governance Conference*, London, July, in *Progressive Politics* (Policy Network), 2:3. Accessed via www. policy-network.net, 7 September 2004.

Coates, D. (2001) 'Capitalist models and social democracy: the case of New Labour', *British Journal of Politics and International Relations*, 3:3 (October): 284–307.

Coates, D. and Lawler, P. (eds) (2000) *New Labour in Power*, Manchester: Manchester University Press.

Coates, K. (ed.) (1999) *The Third Way to the Servile State*, Nottingham: Bertrand Russell Peace Foundation.

Coates, K. and Barratt Brown, M. (1999) 'The Third Way to the servile state', in Coates (ed.), *The Third Way to the Servile State*.

Cockerell, M. (2001) 'An inside view on Blair's Number 10', in Seldon (ed.), *The Blair Effect*.

Coddington, A. and Perryman, M. (eds) (1998) *The Moderniser's Dilemma: Radical Politics in the Age of Blair*, London: Lawrence & Wishart/Signs of the Times.

Collins, H. (2001) 'Is there a Third Way in labour law?', in Giddens (ed.), *The Global Third Way Debate*.

Collins, P. (1996) 'Community, morality and fairness', *Renewal*, 4:3 (July): 32–9.

Commission on Social Justice (1994) *Social Justice: Strategies for National Renewal*, London: Vintage.

Crewe, I. (1988) 'Has the electorate become Thatcherite?', in R. Skidelsky (ed.), *Thatcherism*, London: Chatto & Windus.

Crick, B. (1997) 'Still missing: a public philosophy?', *Political Quarterly*, 68:4 (October): 344–51.

Crouch, C. (1997) 'The terms of the neo-liberal consensus', *Political Quarterly*, 68:4 (October): 352–60.

Crouch, C. (1999) 'The parabola of working class politics', in Gamble and Wright (eds), *The New Social Democracy*.

Crouch, C. (2004) *Post-Democracy*, Cambridge: Polity.

Crouch, C. and Marquand, D. (eds) (1995) *Re-inventing Collective Action: From the Global to the Local*, Oxford: Blackwell for *Political Quarterly*.

Dahrendorf, R. (1999) 'Whatever happened to liberty?', *New Statesman*, 6 September, pp. 25–7.

Davey, K. (1994) 'Waking up to New Times: doubts and dilemmas on the left', in Perryman (ed.), *Altered States*.

Dearlove, J. (2000) 'Globalisation and the study of British politics', *Politics*, 20:2 (May): 111–18.

Democratic Leadership Council (2000) 'The Hyde Park Declaration: a statement of principles and a policy agenda for the 21st century', archived on the DLC website, www.ndol.org.

Desai, M. (2000) 'Still waiting', review of Giddens (2000) *The Third Way and Its Critics*, in *New Times*, April.

Driver, S. and Martell, L. (1997) 'New Labour's communitarianisms', *Critical Social Policy*, 17:3: 27–46.

Driver, S. and Martell, L. (1998) *New Labour: Politics after Thatcherism*, Cambridge: Polity.

Driver, S. and Martell, L. (1999) 'New Labour: culture and economy', in Ray and Sayer (eds), *Culture and Economy after the Cultural Turn*.

Driver, S. and Martell, L. (2000) 'Left, right and the Third Way', *Policy and Politics*, 28:2: 147–61.

Driver, S. and Martell, L. (2002) *Blair's Britain*, Cambridge: Polity.

Eagle, A. (2003) 'A deeper democracy: challenging market fundamentalism', Catalyst working paper, London: Catalyst.

Esping-Andersen, G. (1985) *Politics Against Markets: the Social Democratic Road to Power*, Princeton: Princeton University Press.

Etzioni, A. (2000) *The Third Way to a Good Society*, London: Demos.

Fairclough, N. (2000) *New Labour, New Language?*, London: Routledge.

Faux, J. and Mishel, L. (2000) 'Inequality and the global economy', in Hutton and Giddens (eds), *On the Edge*.

Finlayson, A. (1999) 'Third Way theory', *Political Quarterly*, 70:3 (July): 271–9.

Finlayson, A. (2000) 'New Labour: the culture of government and the government of culture', in Bewes and Gilbert (eds), *Cultural Capitalism*.

Finlayson, A. (2002) 'Elements of the Blairite image of leadership', *Parliamentary Affairs*, 55: 586–99.

Finlayson, A. (2003) *Making Sense of New Labour*, London: Lawrence & Wishart.

Fitzpatrick, T. (2003) *After the New Social Democracy: Social Welfare for the Twenty-First Century*, Manchester: Manchester University Press.

Frankel, B. (1997) 'Confronting neoliberal regimes: the post-Marxist embrace of populism and realpolitik', *New Left Review*, 226 (I) (November–December): 57–92.

Freeden, M. (1999) 'The ideology of New Labour', *Political Quarterly*, 70:1 (January): 42–51.

Freedland, J. (2004) 'Tony Blair's survival is an affront to our constitution', *The Guardian*, 13 September.

Froud, J. *et al.* (1999) 'The Third Way and the jammed economy', *Capital and Class*, 67 (Spring): 155–65.

Gamble, A. (1994) *The Free Economy and the Strong State*, 2nd edition, London: Macmillan.

Gamble, A. and Wright, T. (1999) 'Introduction', in Gamble and Wright (eds), *The New Social Democracy*.

Gamble, A. and Wright, T. (2001) 'From Thatcher to Blair', *Political Quarterly* (January): 1–4.

Gamble, A. and Wright, T. (eds) (1999) *The New Social Democracy*, Oxford: Blackwell.

Garrett, G. (1998) *Partisan Politics in the Global Economy*, Cambridge: Cambridge University Press.

Geras, N. (1987) 'Post-Marxism?', *New Left Review*, 163: 40–82.

Geyer, R. (2003) 'Beyond the Third Way: the science of complexity and the politics of choice', *British Journal of Politics and International Relations*, 5:2 (May): 237–57.

Giddens, A. (1990) *The Consequences of Modernity*, Cambridge: Polity.

Giddens, A. (1994) *Beyond Left and Right: the Future of Radical Politics*, Cambridge: Polity.

Giddens, A. (1998) *The Third Way: the Renewal of Social Democracy*, Cambridge: Polity.

Giddens, A. (2000) *The Third Way and its Critics*, Cambridge: Polity.

Giddens, A. (2001a) 'Introduction', in Giddens (ed.), *The Global Third Way Debate*.

Giddens, A. (2001b) 'The question of inequality', in Giddens (ed.), *The Global Third Way Debate*.

Giddens, A. (2001c) 'Just carry on being new', *New Statesman*, 11 June, pp. 29–31.

Giddens, A. (2002a) *Where Now for New Labour?*, Cambridge: Polity.

Giddens, A. (2002b) 'The third way can beat the far right: by modernising, liberalising and being tough on immigration', www.policy-network.net, 3 May 2002, accessed on 3 July 2002.

Giddens, A. (2003) 'Neoprogessivism: a new agenda for social democracy', in Giddens (ed.), *The Progressive Manifesto*.

Giddens, A. (2004) 'Did they foul up my Third Way?', *New Statesman*, 7 June.

Giddens, A. (ed.) (2001) *The Global Third Way Debate*, Cambridge: Polity.

Giddens, A. (ed.) (2003) *The Progressive Manifesto*, Cambridge: Polity.

Giddens, A. and Hutton, W. (2000) 'In conversation', in Hutton and Giddens (eds), *On the Edge*.

Gilbert, J. (2000a) 'In defence of discourse analysis', in Bewes and Gilbert (eds), *Cultural Capitalism*.

Gilbert, J. (2000b) 'Beyond the hegemony of New Labour', in Bewes and Gilbert (eds), *Cultural Capitalism*.

Gilbert, J. (2004) 'The second wave: the specificity of New Labour neo-liberalism', *Soundings*, 26, pp. 25–45.

Glyn, A. (ed.) (2001) *Social Democracy in Neoliberal Times: the Left and Economic Policy Since 1980*, Oxford: OUP.

Goes, E. (2004) 'The Third Way and the politics of community', in Hale, Leggett and Martell (eds), *The Third Way and Beyond*.

Gould, P. (1999) *The Unfinished Revolution: How the Modernisers saved the Labour Party*, London: Abacus.

Gray, J. (1996) *After Social Democracy: Politics, Capitalism and the Common Life*, London: Demos. Reprinted as chapter 2 in Gray, *Endgames*.

Gray, J. (1997) *Endgames: Questions in Late Modern Political Thought*, Cambridge: Polity.

Greenberg, S. (1990) 'Reconstructing the Democratic vision', *The American Prospect*, 1, Spring.

Habermas, J. (1989) *The Theory of Communicative Action, Lifeworld and System: a Critique of Functionalist Reason, Vol. 2*, Cambridge: Polity.

Hale, S. (2004) 'The communitarian "philosophy" of New Labour', in Hale, Leggett and Martell (eds), *The Third Way and Beyond*.

Hale, S., Leggett, W. and Martell, L. (eds) (2004) *The Third Way and Beyond: Criticisms, Futures, Alternatives*, Manchester: Manchester University Press.

Hall, S. (1988) *The Hard Road to Renewal: Thatcherism and the Crisis of the Left*, London: Verso.

Hall, S. (1997) 'Interview: culture and power', *Radical Philosophy*, 86 (November/December): 24–41.

Hall, S. (1998) 'The great moving nowhere show', *Marxism Today: Special Edition* (November/December).

Hall, S. (2003) 'New Labour's double-shuffle', *Soundings*, 24 (Summer): 10–24.

Hall, S. and Jacques, M. (eds) (1983) *The Politics of Thatcherism*, London: Lawrence & Wishart.

Hall, S. and Jacques, M. (eds) (1989) *New Times: the Changing Face of Politics in the 1990s*, London: Lawrence & Wishart.

Halpern, D. and Mikosz, D. (eds) (1998) *The Third Way: Summary of the NEXUS On-Line Discussion*, London: Nexus.

Hargreaves, I. and Christie, I. (eds) (1998) *Tomorrow's Politics: the Third Way and Beyond*, London: Demos.

Hattersley, R. (1987) *Choose Freedom*, London: Michael Joseph.

Hay, C. (1999) *The Political Economy of New Labour: Labouring under False Pretences?*, Manchester: Manchester University Press.

Hay, C. and Watson, M. (1999) 'Globalisation: "sceptical" notes on the 1999 Reith Lectures', *Political Quarterly*, 70:4 (October): 418–25.

Heath, A., Jowell, R. and Curtice, J. (eds) (2001) *The Rise of New Labour: Party Policies and Voter Choices*, Oxford: Oxford University Press.

Heffernan, R. (1996) 'Accounting for New Labour: the impact of Thatcherism, 1979–1995', *Contemporary Political Studies*, 3:3.

Heffernan, R. (2000) *New Labour and Thatcherism: Political Change in Britain*, Basingstoke: Palgrave – now Palgrave Macmillan.

Held, D. (1998) 'The timid tendency', *Marxism Today: Special Edition* (November/December).

Held, D. (2001) 'Regulating globalization? The reinvention of politics', in Giddens (ed.), *The Global Third Way Debate*.

Held, D. (2003) 'Global social democracy', in Giddens (ed.), *The Progressive Manifesto*.

Held, D. (2004) *Global Covenant*, Cambridge: Polity.

Hirst, P. (1997) *From Statism to Pluralism: Democracy, Civil Society and Global Politics*, London: Routledge.

Hirst, P. (1999a) 'Globalisation and social democracy', in Gamble and Wright (eds), *The New Social Democracy*.

Hirst, P. (1999b) 'The strange death of New Labour England?', *Renewal*, 7:4 (Autumn): 9–15.

Hirst, P. and Bader, V. (eds) (2001) *Associative Democracy: the Real Third Way*, London: Frank Cass.

Hirst, P. and Thompson, G. (1996) *Globalization in Question*, Cambridge: Polity.

Hobsbawm, E. (1998) 'The death of neo-liberalism', *Marxism Today: Special Edition* (November/December): 4–8.

Hoggart, S. (1999) 'No joke for No.10 when a Hague gag hits the target', *The Guardian*, 11 November.

Hombach, B. (2000) *The Politics of the New Centre*, Cambridge: Polity.

Hutton, W. (1995) *The State We're In*, London: Jonathan Cape.

Hutton, W. (1997) *The State to Come*, London: Vintage.

Hutton, W. and Giddens, A. (eds) (2000) *On the Edge: Living with Global Capitalism*, London: Jonathan Cape.

Institute for Public Policy Research (2004) *The State of the Nation: an Audit of Injustice in the UK*, London: IPPR.

Jacobs, M. (1999) 'Environmental democracy', in Gamble and Wright (eds), *The New Social Democracy*.

Jacobs, M. (2001) 'The environment, modernity and the Third Way', in Giddens (ed.), *The Global Third Way Debate*.

Jacques, M. (2004) 'He risks leading his party into an electoral wilderness', *The Guardian*, 20 July.

Jacques, M. (ed.) (1998) *Marxism Today: Special Edition* (November/December).

Jordan, B. (2001) 'Globalization, exclusion and progressive economic policies', in Tam (ed.), *Progressive Politics in the Global Age*.

Kapstein, E.B. (1999) 'The Third Way and the international order', in Giddens (ed.), *The Global Third Way Debate*.

Kelly, G., Kelly, D. and Gamble, A. (eds) (1997) *Stakeholder Capitalism*, London: Macmillan.

King, A. (1999) 'Legitimating Post-Fordism: a critique of Anthony Giddens' later works', *Telos*, 115 (Spring): 61–77.

Kircheimer, O. (1966) 'The transformation of the Western European party systems', extract published in Martell and Outhwaite (eds), *The Sociology of Politics*.

Krieger, J. (1999) *British Politics in the Global Age: Can Social Democracy Survive?*, Cambridge: Polity.

Laclau, E. (1990) *New Reflections on the Revolution of our Time*, London: Verso.

Laclau, E. and Mouffe, C. (1990) 'Post-Marxism without apologies', in Laclau, *New Reflections on the Revolution of our Time*.

Lafontaine, O. (2000) *The Heart Beats on the Left*, Cambridge: Polity.

Larkin, P. (2000) 'New Labour and old revisionism', *Renewal*, 8:1 (Winter): 42–9.

Latham, M. (2001) 'The Third Way: an outline', in Giddens (ed.), *The Global Third Way Debate*.

Lawson, N. *et al.* (2004) '(Not) as good as it gets', *Renewal*, 12:3. Accessed via www.renewal.org.uk.

Lawson, N. and Sherlock, N. (eds) (2001) *The Progressive Century: the Future of the Centre-Left in Britain*, Basingstoke: Palgrave – now Palgrave Macmillan.

Le Grand, J. (1998) 'The Third Way begins with CORA', *New Statesman*, 6 March.

Leadbeater, C. (2004) 'Third Way on the beach', *Prospect*, August.

Leggett, W. (2000) 'New Labour's Third Way: from "New Times" to "no choice", *Studies in Social and Political Thought*, 3, September, pp. 19–31.

Leggett, W. (2002) 'Reflexive modernization and reconstructing the Third Way: a response to Mouzelis', *The Sociological Review*, 50:3, August, pp. 419–36.

Leggett, W. (2004a) 'Criticism and the future of the Third Way' in Hale, Leggett and Martell (eds), *The Third Way and Beyond*.

Leggett, W. (2004b) 'Social change, values and political agency: the case of the Third Way', *Politics*, 24:1 (February): 12–19.

Lent, A. (1994) 'Radical democracy: arguments and principles' in Perryman (ed.), *Altered States*.

Lester, J. (2000) 'Common sense, reality and the Third Way: The illusion of an alternative to neoliberalism', paper presented at the National Autonomous University of Mexico, 10–13 April.

Levitas, R. (1998) *The Inclusive Society? Social Exclusion and New Labour*, Basingstoke: Macmillan – now Palgrave Macmillan.

Levitas, R. (2004) 'Shuffling back to equality?, *Soundings*, 26, pp. 59–72.

Lister, R. (2001) 'Towards an inclusive society: from social exclusion to social justice', Social Science Forum Annual Lecture, University of Brighton, 10 May.

Little, A. (2002) 'Community and radical democracy', *Journal of Political Ideologies*, 7:3: 369–82.

Ludlam, S. and Smith, M.J. (eds) (2001) *New Labour in Government*, Manchester: Manchester University Press.

Ludlam, S. and Smith, M.J. (eds) (2004) *Governing as New Labour: Policy and Politics under Blair*, Basingstoke: Palgrave – now Palgrave Macmillan.

McCullen, P. and Harris, C. (2004) 'Generative equality, work and the Third Way: a managerial perspective', in Hale, Leggett and Martell (eds), *The Third Way and Beyond*.

McLennan, G. (2004) 'Travelling with vehicular ideas: the case of the Third Way', *Economy and Society*, 33:4 (November): 484–99.

Mair, P. (2000) 'Partyless democracy: solving the paradox of New Labour?', *New Left Review*, 2 (March/April): 21–35.

Mandelson, P. (2002) [1996] *The Blair Revolution Revisited*, London: Politicos.

Marcuse, H. (1964) *One-Dimensional Man: Studies in the Ideology of Advanced Industrial Society*, London: Routledge.

Marquand, D. (1989) 'Beyond left and right: the need for a new politics', in Hall and Jacques (eds), *New Times*.

Marquand, D. (1991) *The Progressive Dilemma*, London: Heinemann.

Marquand, D. (1999a) 'Premature obsequies: social democracy comes in from the cold', in Gamble and Wright (eds), *The New Social Democracy*.

Marquand, D. (1999b) 'Pluralism v populism', *Prospect* (June): 27–31.

Marquand, D. (2004) *Decline of the Public*, Cambridge: Polity.

Martell, L. and Outhwaite, W. (eds) (1998) *The Sociology of Politics, vol. 2*, Cheltenham: Edward Elgar.

Martell, L. *et al.* (eds) (2001) *Social Democracy: Global and National Perspectives*, Basingstoke: Palgrave – now Palgrave Macmillan.

Meredith, S. (2003) 'New Labour: "the road less travelled"?', *Politics*, 23:3 (September): 163–71.

Meredyth, D. and Minson, J. (eds) (2001) *Citizenship and Cultural Policy*, London: Sage.

Merkel, W. (2001) 'The Third Ways of social democracy', in Giddens (ed.), *The Global Third Way Debate*.

Midgley, J. (1999) 'Growth, redistribution and welfare: toward social investment', in Giddens (ed.), *The Global Third Way Debate*.

Milburn, A. (2005) 'Labour's contract for a third term', *The Guardian*, 15 January.

Miliband, D. (1994) 'Introduction', in Miliband (ed.), *Reinventing the Left*.

Miliband, D. (ed.) (1994) *Reinventing the Left*, Cambridge: Polity.

Miliband, R. (1994) *Socialism for a Sceptical Age*, Cambridge: Polity.

Morris, D. (1997) *Behind the Oval Office: Winning the Presidency in the Nineties*, New York: Random House.

Morrison, D. (2004) 'New Labour, citizenship and the discourse of the Third Way', in Hale, Leggett and Martell (eds), *The Third Way and Beyond*.

Mouffe, C. (1992) *Dimensions of Radical Democracy*, London: Verso.

Mouffe, C. (1998) 'The radical centre: a politics without adversary', *Soundings*, 9 (Summer).

Mouffe, C. (1999) '10 years of false starts', *New Times*, 18 November.

Mouffe, C. (2000) *The Democratic Paradox*, London: Verso.

Mouzelis, N. (2001) 'Reflexive modernization and the third way: the impasses of Giddens' social-democratic politics', *The Sociological Review*, 49:3 (August): 436–56.

Mulgan, G. (1989) 'Uncertainty, reversibility and variety', in Hall and Jacques (eds), *New Times*.

Mulgan, G. (1997) *Connexity: How to Live in a Connected World*, London: Random House.

Mulgan, G. (ed.) (1997) *Life After Politics: New Thinking for the Twenty-First Century*, London: Fontana for *Demos*.

Mulgan, G. and Briscoe, I. (1997) 'The society of networks: a new form of organisation for the information age', in Mulgan (ed.), *Life After Politics*.

Needham, C. (2004) 'Customer-focused government', *Soundings*, 26, pp. 73–85.

Newman, J. (2001) *Modernising Governance: New Labour, Policy and Society*, London: Sage.

Newman, O. and de Zoysa, R. (2001) *The Promise of the Third Way: Globalization and Social Justice*, Basingstoke: Palgrave – now Palgrave Macmillan.

O'Brien, M. *et al.* (eds) (1999) *Theorising Modernity*, Harlow: Addison, Wesley, Longman.

Perryman, M. (ed.) (1994) *Altered States: Postmodernism, Politics, Culture*, London: Lawrence & Wishart/Signs of the Times.

Perryman, M. (ed.) (1996) *The Blair Agenda*, London: Lawrence & Wishart.

Phillips, L. (1998) 'Hegemony and political discourse: the lasting impact of Thatcherism', *Sociology*, 32:4: 847–67.

Philo, G. (1994) 'Politics, media and public belief', in Perryman (ed.), *Altered States*.

Pierson, C. (2001) *Hard Choices: Social Democracy in the 21st Century*, Cambridge: Polity.

Prideaux, S. (2004) 'From organisational theory to the Third Way: continuities and contradictions underpinning Amitai Etzioni's communitarian influence on New Labour', in Hale, Leggett and Martell (eds), *The Third Way and Beyond*.

Przeworski, A. (2001) 'How many ways can be third?', in Glyn (ed.), *Social Democracy in Neoliberal Times*.

Rawnsley, A. (2002) 'New Labour grows up', *The Observer*, 21 April.

Ray, L. and Sayer, A. (eds) (1999) *Culture and Economy after the Cultural Turn*, London: Sage.

Rose, N. (1999a) *Powers of Freedom: Reframing Political Thought*, Cambridge: Cambridge University Press.

Rose, N. (1999b) 'Inventiveness in politics', *Economy and Society*, 28:3 (August): 467–93.

Rose, N. (2001) 'Community, citizenship and the Third Way', in Meredyth and Minson (eds), *Citizenship and Cultural Policy*.

Rose, N. and Miller, P. (1992) 'Political power beyond the state: problematics of government', *British Journal of Sociology*, 43:2: 173–205.

Rubinstein, D. (1997) 'How new is New Labour?', *Political Quarterly*, 68:4: 339–43.

Rubinstein, D. (2000) 'A new look at New Labour', *Politics*, 20:3 (September) 161–7.

Rustin, M. (1994) 'Unfinished business – from Thatcherite modernisation to incomplete modernity', in Perryman (ed.), *Altered States*.

Rustin, M. (1995) 'The future of post-socialism', *Radical Philosophy*, 74 (November/December): 17–27.

Rustin, M. (2001) 'The third sociological way', in *op. cit.* eds. Arestis and Sawyer (2001).

Salvati, M. (2001) 'Prolegomena to the Third Way debate', in White (ed.), *New Labour*.

Seldon, A. (ed.) (2001) *The Blair Effect: the Blair Government 1997–2001*, London: Little, Brown and Co.

Selznick, P. (2001) 'A quest for community', in Tam (ed.), *Progressive Politics in the Global Age*.

Seyd, P. and Whitely, P. (2001) 'New Labour and the Party: members and organization', in Ludlam and Smith (eds), *New Labour in Government*.

Shaw, E. (1994) *The Labour Party Since 1979: Crisis and Transformation*, London: Routledge.

Shaw, E. (2004) 'What matters is what works: the Third Way and the case of the Private Finance Initiative', in Hale, Leggett and Martell (eds), *The Third Way and Beyond*.

Showstack Sassoon, A. (1998) 'From realism to creativity – Gramsci, Blair and us', in Coddington and Perryman (eds), *The Moderniser's Dilemma*.

Sklair, L. (2001) *The Transnational Capitalist Class*, Oxford: Blackwell.

Smith, C. (1996) *New Questions for Socialism*, Fabian Society Pamphlet 577, London: College Hill.

Tam, H. (ed.) (2001) *Progressive Politics in the Global Age*, Cambridge: Polity.

Taylor-Gooby, P. (1997) 'In defence of second-best theory: state, class and capital in social policy', *Journal of Social Policy*, 26:2: 171–92.

Terranova, T. (2000) 'Of systems and networks: digital regeneration and the pragmatics of postmodern knowledge', in Bewes and Gilbert (eds), *Cultural Capitalism*.

Thompson, P. and Gould, P. (2003) 'Thompson vs. Gould: is New Labour still new?', *Renewal*, 11:1. Accessed via www.renewal.org.uk, 3 November 2004.

Touraine, A. (2001) *Beyond Neoliberalism*, Cambridge: Polity.

Toynbee, P. (2004) 'Blair trashed the 60s for the sake of a Tory one-liner', *The Guardian*, 21 July.

Vandenbroucke, F. (1998) *Globalisation, Inequality and Social Democracy*, London: IPPR.

Vandenbroucke, F. (2001) 'European social democracy and the Third Way: convergence, divisions and shared questions', in White (ed.), *New Labour*.

Vincent, A. (1998) 'New ideologies for old?', *Political Quarterly*, 69:1 (January): 48–58.

Watkins, S. (2004) 'A weightless hegemony: New Labour's role in the neoliberal order', *New Left Review*, 25: 5–33.

Webb, P. and Fisher, J. (2003) 'Professionalism and the Millbank tendency: the political sociology of New Labour's employees', *Politics*, 23:1 (February): 10–20.

Wenman, M.A. (2003) 'What is politics? The approach of radical pluralism', *Politics*, 23:1 (February): 57–65.

Westergaard, J. (1999) 'Where does the third way lead?', *New Political Economy*, 4:3: 429–36.

White, S. (1998) 'Interpreting the "third way": not one road, but many', *Renewal*, 6:2 (Spring).

White, S. (1999a) 'Rights and responsibilities': a social democratic perspective', in Gamble and Wright (eds), *The New Social Democrary*.

White, S. (1999b) 'Social liberalism, stakeholder socialism and post-industrial social democracy', *Renewal*, 7:4 (Autumn): 29–38.

White, S. (2001) 'The ambiguities of the Third Way', in White (ed.), *New Labour*.

White, S. (ed.) (2001) *New Labour: the Progressive Future?*, Basingstoke: Palgrave – now Palgrave Macmillan.

Wickham-Jones, M. (2000) 'New Labour in the global economy: partisan politics and the democratic model', *British Journal of Politics and International
Relations*, 2:1 (April): 1–25.

Wilson, R. (1999) 'Liberal socialism and the future of progressive politics',
Renewal, 7:4 (Autumn): 16–28.

Wood, B. (1998) 'Stuart Hall's cultural studies and the problem of hegemony',
British Journal of Sociology, 49:3 (September): 399–414.

Woodiwiss, A. (1997) 'Against "modernity": a dissident rant', *Economy and
Society*, 26:1 (February): 1–21.

Wright, T. (1997a) *Why Vote Labour?*, London: Penguin.

Wright, T. (1997b) *Who Dares Wins: New Labour – New Politics*, Fabian
Pamphlet, 579, London: Fabian Society.

Wright, T. (2001) 'Liberal socialism: then and now', in Lawson and Sherlock
(eds), *The Progressive Century*.

Index